A Life of Balance

Nuggets for a Successful Walk with God

Alison Chant

A Life of Balance

Nuggets for a Successful Walk with God

Alison Chant

Copyright Worldwide © 2020 by Alison Chant

ISBN 978-1-61529-225-7

All rights reserved worldwide

No part of this book may be reproduced in any manner without the written permission of the author except in brief quotes embodied in critical articles or reviews.

Vision Publishing
P.O. Box 1680
Ramona, CA 92065
1 (760) 789- 4700
www.booksbyvision.org

All scripture quotes from the New International Version unless otherwise stated.

Other books by Alison Chant

Unsung Heroines – Author and Editor

Divine Healing – The Wonder and the Mystery

Walking in the Spirit

Cameos of Christ

The History of Vision

Table of Contents

Foreword 5
Preface 7
Chapter One: A Good Foundation 9
Chapter Two: Workers, Worshippers and Warriors 27
Chapter Three: How We Speak To God 43
Chapter Four: How God Speaks To Us 55
Chapter Five: Champions / Overcomers 69
Chapter Six: Encouragement 89
Chapter Seven: Jesus Cares for You 99
Chapter Eight: The Seeds of Faith 109
Chapter Nine: In the Garden of God 121
Chapter Ten: Jonah's Trials 137
Chapter Eleven: The Path To Victory 147
Chapter Twelve: Creative Thoughts 159
Chapter Thirteen: Winning by Losing 169
Chapter Fourteen: After God's Heart 179
Chapter Fifteen: Character and Discipline 187
Chapter Sixteen: The Pillars of Solomon 197
Bibliography 205

Foreword

This book, *A Life of Balance- Nuggets for a Successful Walk with God,* is a *transformation* prescription for success, *balance*, or stability, in Christian life, which can only be found in a deep knowledge of Jesus Christ. It is spiritual food for the soul.

If we love God, Body, Soul, Spirit, and Strength, we obey and apply his instructions, which results in victories and successes. Throughout the Bible, God said to his people: "If you will do, I will do as well; and if you don't, I won't ..." So, the book speaks about following his instructions and his response to obedience, which will bring God's blessings; or, if people disobey, his curses. Sadly, God's chosen people often try to obey in their own strength, which always results in failure, while the Holy Spirit teaches us to hide his word in our hearts so that we won't sin against him (Psalm 119). As a result, it is in the strength of the Lord that we can do all things.

When we surrender to *The Great Physician*, he brings Divine Healing to us – in Body, Soul, and Spirit. He is the answer to whatever the need is, and he reveals himself to those who diligently seek him. The God who cares brings healing and transformation to our lives when we apply his Word.

Alison, who is a Spiritual Mother to many, has a unique approach to leading God-seekers step-by-step on a spiritual journey of discovery of God. In the process, she causes us to look at self in a realistic and honest way. When we seek God with our whole heart, we discover a loving and caring God who is well-pleased in those who delight in him.

This inspiring book will motivate God's children to become a people ready to do whatever it takes to come to a place of knowing him in an intimate and personal way.

Another of Alison's books, *Divine Healing, The Wonder and the Mystery*, was an inspiration to our congregation and to our School of Ministry. The result was many miracles and testimonies. It made a difference in the lives of those who believed and received, raising a new level of faith.

Without a doubt, this new book, *A Life of Balance- Nuggets for a Successful Walk with God,* is also a life-transforming prescription.

Senior Pastor Dr. Manon Gurley

Tabernacle Church. Laurel.

Preface

Recently I began to meditate on what it really means to love God with all your heart, soul, mind and strength. From that thought arose many other thoughts, some of which I have included in this book. I trust that you will benefit from the ideas I have uncovered and that you will understand a little more of what it means to love the Lord your God with all that lies within you.

We find in scripture God's principles on which to build a stable Christian life. A life that is neither hyper spiritual and fanatical on the one hand, nor less than spiritual; lacking in prayer and the reading of the Word, on the other. Between the two there remains a balanced, strong and decisive Christian life which is pleasing to the Lord. My hope is that you will agree with my findings and enjoy this kind of life continuing to love the Lord with all your heart, soul, mind and strength and your neighbour as yourself.

Alison Chant

Chapter One:

A Good Foundation

How can we lead a balanced Christian life? What basic principles do we need to follow? Let us begin with the most important foundation of all: *"loving God with all your heart, soul, mind and strength."*

Do you remember how you felt when you first accepted Jesus as your Saviour? How much you enjoyed reading the Bible, and how you looked forward to each church meeting? Do you remember that nothing was more important at that time than learning all you could about being a Christian and pleasing God in all that you were doing?

Speaking to the church at Ephesus Jesus rebukes them for forsaking their first love for him –

> "But this is what I have against you; you do not love me now as you did at first. Think how far you have fallen! Turn from your sins and do what you did at first. If you don't turn from your sins, I will come to you and take your lampstand from its place" (Re 2:4-5; GNB).

It is a good idea to take stock of your life every now and then and to ask yourself these questions: Do I still have the same enthusiasm and the same excitement about Christian life as I did when I first believed? Do I love the Word of God and the fellowship of the saints as much as I did when I first became a Christian? Have I allowed other things to enter my life which take more of my time than the study of God's Word? Do I love God with my whole heart, soul, mind and strength?

A memory: In the year 1949 when I was fifteen years of age my older brother James and I attended a regular Friday night prayer meeting at the home of Mrs Batts, a member of the Adelaide *National Revival Crusade*[1] pastored by Leo Harris. Along with about 25 others we crowded into her tiny lounge room and prayed for revival and for the Baptism of the Holy Spirit with signs following. After these meetings James and I found it hard to tear ourselves away from listening to our friends who enjoyed talking about different aspects of the Bible which were all new and exciting to us.

This was the year after Israel had become a nation and four years after the Second World War had ended, with the atom bomb destroying Hiroshima and Nagasaki. Bible prophecy indicated that these two historic developments could be signs of the imminent return of Christ. Constantly, week after week, we were so caught up in this and other discussions that we waited too long to catch the last bus to our suburb of Panorama. In those days hardly anyone owned a car so if you missed your bus or train you had to walk. We were five miles from our family home, but we thought nothing of the journey. We were so caught up in the wonder of our relationship with the Lord we continued to talk together about the Word of God as we walked home. This is a precious memory and one that gives me one way of measuring my love for the Lord many decades later.

Jesus' teaching: When asked by a teacher of the law which was the most important commandment -

> "The most important one," answered Jesus, "is this: 'Hear: O Israel: The Lord our God, the Lord is one. Love the Lord your God with all your heart and with all your soul and with all your mind and with all your strength.' The second is this: 'Love your neighbour as yourself.' There is no commandment greater than these" (Mk 12:29-31).

---

[1] The original name of the *CRC Churches International* movement.

Loving God with all your heart: The heart contains the emotional or moral nature, as distinguished from the intellectual nature of man.[2]

There are many scriptures with reference to the heart, pointing to all aspects of our human condition. Here are some of them -

> "The Lord does not look at the things people look at. People look at the outward appearance, but the LORD looks at the heart" (1 Sa 16:7b).

> "I have hidden your word in my heart; that I might not sin against you" (Ps 119: 11).

> "Search me, God, and know my heart; test me and know my anxious thoughts" (Ps 139:23).

> "Create in me a pure heart, O God, and renew a steadfast spirit within me" (Ps 51:10).

> "Blessed are the pure in heart, for they will see God" (Mt 5:8).

When purity is lost –

> "What comes out of a person is what defiles them. For it is from within, out of a person's heart, that evil thoughts come" (Mk 7:20-21a).

> "To the pure, all things are pure, but to those who are corrupted and do not believe, nothing is pure. In fact, both their minds and consciences are corrupted" (Tit 1:15).

It is extremely hard today, to keep our minds pure because of the evil that is so rampant in our society. Some, though by no

---

[2] Webster's *New Collegiate Dictionary*; G & C Merriam Co. Springfield, Massachusetts; 1980.

means all, of the things we see on television, in magazines, and films, as well as the evil of pornography have drawn many people down into a cesspool of filth.

To protect ourselves, we Christians must be very careful of what we allow our eyes to see and our ears to hear. We can do much to protect ourselves, and we should do what we can.

Heart memories: Do the verses in scripture concerning the heart mean our physical heart has some memory apart from our brain? It seems sure that the heart holds at least some of our memories!

Those who have had heart transplants have had strange dreams, and feelings that they did not have before. Paul Pearsall presents a number of these stories in his book *The Heart's Code*.[3]

Indeed, according to modern medical science, all the muscles in our body have some memory.

Attitudes of the heart: There are some attitudes that can stop us from loving God with all our heart, such as **bitterness -**

> "See to it that no one falls short of the grace of God and that no bitter root grows up to cause trouble and defile many" (He 12:15).

Bitter roots are planted when we hold a judgment against someone in our heart. They can grow from negative words said to you, such as, "You will never amount to anything;" or sinful actions done to you, actions you resent and find hard to forgive.

---

[3] *The Heart's Code, Tapping the Wisdom and Power of Our Heart's Energy* by Paul P. Pearsall

Or perhaps even from negative or sinful acts done by you; actions you now bitterly regret.

If we hold bitter judgments, then we reap what we have sown. Bitter roots can control our life and our relationships -

> "Do not be deceived: God cannot be mocked. A man reaps what he sows" (Ga 6:7).

- **Bitter roots can affect how we see things.** Our minds can be twisted to point in the wrong direction, and if we persist in looking at things the wrong way, this can lead on to a paranoid reaction.

- **Bitter roots can affect our attitudes**; causing us to react to others by getting angry very easily, and anger destroys relationships.

- **Bitter roots can affect our behaviour.** We can destroy close friendships by passing on the negative, accusing words spoken to us in the past.[4]

How can we escape from these bitter roots?

We must confess: Freedom comes through confession! Whether we are the one at fault, or the victim, we need to repent, otherwise we are in prison, bound to the past -

> "Confess your sins to each other and pray for each other so that you may be healed. The prayer of a righteous person is powerful and effective" (Ja 5:16).

Even though this verse is originally for healing of the body it is also true for healing of negative heart emotions which can bind us to the past.

---

[4] These Bitter Roots and how they affect us come from notes provided by Sister Arlene Liang; Registered Mental Health Nurse.

We must forgive: We need to forgive any who have hurt us and there are at least three reasons why we should forgive –

- **It is required by God –**

"When you stand praying, if you hold anything against anyone, forgive them, so that your Father in heaven may forgive you your sins" (Mk 11:25).

- **To avoid entrapment by Satan** – Paul advises the Corinthian church -

"Anyone you forgive, I also forgive. And what I have forgiven – if there was anything to forgive – I have forgiven in the sight of Christ for your sake, <u>in order that Satan might not outwit us. For we are not unaware of his schemes</u>" (2 Co 2:10-11).

- **And because forgiveness should come naturally to God's children.**

"Bear with each other and forgive one another if any of you has a grievance against someone. Forgive as the Lord forgave you" (Co 3:13

If you find it hard to forgive then ask God for help. Put yourself in his hands and tell him you are willing for him to help you to forgive when necessary! This attitude allows the Holy Spirit to work in you to accomplish your act of forgiveness.

Other hindrances: There are other things that can hinder us from loving God with our whole heart, such as **fear, anxiety and depression.**

Over three hundred times in the Bible we are encouraged not to be afraid. Anxiety and depression are many times the result of a lack of trust in the loving kindness of God -

"Do not be anxious about anything, but in every situation, by prayer and petition, with thanksgiving, present your requests to God. And the peace of God, which transcends all understanding, will guard your hearts and your minds in Christ Jesus" (Ph 4:6-7).

How can we love God with our whole being if we are not trusting him fully to care for us and keep us in his love? We must trust him absolutely.

Living by God's principles: If we want to love God with all our heart, then we also need to learn to live by God's principles and change all our old thinking for new. As we read and meditate on God's Word it is powerful enough to cleanse our mind and our heart.

We can learn these principles of God from the teachings of Jesus in the gospels. We should study them carefully and make sure we live by them.

Then we can go on to love God with a whole heart, cleansed and furnished with the fruits of the Spirit – "*Love, joy, peace, forbearance, kindness, goodness, faithfulness, gentleness and self- control*" (Ga 5:22).

Loving God with your soul: The soul is the spiritual part of a person; the part of a person that does not die, but there is some difficulty in speaking of the soul without the spirit. Here are some scriptures to illustrate this -

> "The LORD is my Shepherd, I lack nothing. He makes me lie down in green pastures, he leads me beside quiet waters, he refreshes my soul" (Ps 23:1-3).

> "Come to me, all you who are weary and burdened, and I will give you rest. Take my yoke upon you and learn from me, for I am gentle and humble in heart, and you will find rest for your souls. For my yoke is easy and my burden is light" (Mt 11:28-29).

> "Then the LORD God formed a man from the dust of the ground and breathed into his nostrils the breath of life, and man became a living being" (Ge 2:7).
>
> "The LORD who stretches out the heavens, who lays the foundation of the earth, and who forms the human spirit within a person..." (Zec 12:1)

There is some difference between them, but the preference by most scholars is to view them as one and the same. Joined as one, they are that part of us that lives forever after we die.

> **According to Vine's Dictionary:** "The language of the verse in Hebrews 4:12 ... "For the Word of God is alive and active. Sharper than any double-edged sword, it penetrates even to dividing soul and spirit, joints and marrow; it judges the thoughts and attitudes of the heart"...suggests the extreme difficulty of distinguishing between the soul and the spirit, alike in their nature and in their activities.
>
> **Vine continues:** "Generally speaking, the spirit is the higher, the soul the lower element. The spirit may be recognised as the life principle bestowed on man by God, the soul as the resulting life constituted in the individual, the body being the material organism animated by soul and spirit."[5]

The following references can indicate both the soul and the spirit -

> "Your beauty should not come from outward adornment...Rather, it should be that of your inner self, the unfading beauty of a gentle and quiet spirit, which is of great worth in God's sight" (1 Pe 3:3a & 4).

---

[5] Vine's Expository Dictionary of New Testament Words. Volume 4 Page 54

"I pray that out of his glorious riches he may strengthen you with power through his Spirit in your <u>inner being,</u> so that Christ may dwell in your hearts through faith" (Ep 3:16-17a).

Loving God with all our soul is proved by allowing him to refresh and strengthen our inner self, so that we can continue growing in grace, becoming more like Jesus every day.

A meditation on the butterfly: The metamorphosis of the Monarch butterfly can illustrate in some ways the mystery of soul and spirit. The caterpillar being likened to our human body, and the creative changes going on within the chrysalis formed by the caterpillar, illustrating the soul and spirit merging into a beautiful new creation.

There is a fascination in the life cycle of the Monarch butterfly. It begins with an egg planted by the adult butterfly on a leaf of the plant it prefers. When the egg hatches it becomes a caterpillar that grows steadily until, shedding and renewing its skin several times, it reaches adulthood. It then forms a chrysalis around itself which attaches to a tree branch. Inside the chrysalis, over a period of fifteen days, the elements which made up the caterpillar move around, rearranging the molecules, until a miracle occurs and the adult butterfly emerges – a creature so beautiful and so changed from its original form that it seems impossible the two elements have come from the same origin.[6]

One day when the Lord Jesus returns to this world, we will be caught up to meet him, transformed from this realm to an eternal life in him. Our inner new creation will be revealed; we shall be like Jesus -

---

[6] A film on the metamorphosis of the Monarch butterfly can be seen on Wikipedia.

"Dear friends, now we are children of God, and what we will be has not yet been made known. But we know that when Christ appears, we shall be like him, for we shall see him as he is" (1 Jn 3:2)

Loving God with your mind: The mind is the element or complex of elements in an individual that feels, perceives, thinks, wills, and especially reasons.[7]

In the command to love God the word for mind is (Greek) *dianoia,* "lit. a thinking through, or over, a meditation, reflecting, signifies (a) the faculty of knowing, understanding, or moral reflection."[8]

The Berean Jews, after hearing the gospel from Paul – "received the message with great eagerness and examined the Scriptures every day to see if what Paul said was true" (Ac 17:11b).

The Jews in Berea were using their minds, thinking through what they had been told, meditating and reflecting on what Paul had preached about Jesus being the Messiah for whom they had been waiting. We too should use our minds to examine the truth concerning Jesus.

"Therefore, with minds that are alert and fully sober, set your hope on the grace to be brought to you when Jesus Christ is revealed at his coming" (1Pe 1:13).

It is with our minds we meditate on God's Word and make the decision to believe and receive his promises.

Think about God: Take a familiar verse such as John 3:16 and meditate on it carefully, expanding it beyond the obvious words, thus –

---

[7] Websters Dictionary
[8] Vine's Expository Dictionary of NT Words. Vol.3 page 69.

God: The marvellous and wonderful Creator who dwells in light inaccessible. In him is no shadow of turning. He says of himself that he is loving, gracious, kind, slow to anger, and forgiving (see Ge 1:1; Ex 34:6; Ja 1:16).

So loved: He is a God of love, unconditional and universal. He loves everyone, no matter our condition, or our race. We are each one precious to him, worth more than all the world (see 1 Jn 3:1).

The world: The world as in the whole complex of civilisation, the people that make up the teeming multitudes of mankind. He loves each of us with a deep and steadfast love which can't be shaken (see 1 Jn 4:7-10).

That he gave: He is a giving God, so generous and kind. He gives life even to those who turn away from his love, even those who refuse to believe he exists. He could take away their breath in an instant, but instead he is longsuffering and sends his rain on the just and the unjust (see Ro 5:6-8; Mt 5:45).

His one and only Son: Here is such love and condescension toward us mere mortals, that our great God should be willing to send Jesus, his one and only Son, into our little world to suffer and die that we might live. What overwhelming kindness! Without this we would be lost and undone with no hope for the future (see Is 53).

That whoever believes in him: Such a simple statement. It leaves no one behind. How grateful we should be that God has made it possible for the simplest soul to reach out and grasp the salvation he has planned, just by believing in Jesus and accepting the rescue he has purchased for us by his precious sacrifice (see Ro 10:9-10).

Shall not perish but have eternal life: What a wonderful promise, to gain eternal life, the very life of God himself. What a privilege for those who believe, to be saved from destruction, to live forever with the Lord. To spend eternity praising and worshiping Jesus while working to complete the will of the Father. What a wonderful and exciting future we have in store for us (see Jn 17:1-3; Re 7:9-17).

We must search the Word: To love God with all our mind we must search his Word diligently; being careful to learn all we can about him.

He is sovereign, he is all wise; he is all powerful and he is everywhere present, but he is much more still:

He revealed himself to Moses on Mount Sanai: He passed in front of Moses, proclaiming -

> "The LORD, the LORD, the compassionate and gracious God, slow to anger, abounding in love and faithfulness, maintaining love to thousands, and forgiving wickedness, rebellion and sin. Yet he does not leave the guilty unpunished; he punishes the children and their children for the sin of the parents to the third and fourth generation" (Ex 34:6-7)

He also revealed himself to Moses as a jealous God -

> "I, the LORD your God, am a jealous God, punishing the children for the sin of the parents to the third and fourth generation of those who hate me, but showing love to a thousand generations of those who love me and keep my commandments" Ex 20:5b-6)

> "Do not worship any other god, for the Lord, whose name is Jealous, is a jealous God" (34:14).

God is even more than these -

He is also just – "He is the Rock, his works are perfect, and all his ways are just. A faithful God who does no wrong, upright and just is he" (De 32:4)

He is accepting – "The Lord your God is with you, the Mighty Warrior who saves. He will take great delight in you; in his love he will no longer rebuke you but will rejoice over you with singing" (Zep 3:17).

He is affectionate – "You, Lord, are forgiving and good, abounding in love to all who call to you" (Ps 86:5).

He is a helper – "God is our refuge and strength, an ever-present help in trouble". (Ps 46:1).

He communicates – "I sought the LORD, and he answered me; he delivered me from all my fears" (Ps. 34:4).

He is generous – "For God so loved the world that gave his one and only Son, that whoever believes in him shall not perish but have eternal life" (Jn 3:16).

He knows everything – "Nothing in all creation is hidden from God's sight. Everything is uncovered and laid bare before the eyes of him to whom we must give account" (He 4:13).

He disciplines – "My son, do not make light of the Lord's discipline, and do not lose heart when he rebukes you, because the Lord disciplines the one he loves, and he chastens everyone he accepts as his son" (12:5b-6).

Jesus came to show us God in human flesh - a wise, loving, compassionate God who heals and delivers and wants the very best for us -

> "When he saw the crowds, he had compassion on them, because they were harassed and helpless, like sheep without a shepherd" (Mt 9:36).

> "God anointed Jesus of Nazareth with the Holy Spirit and power, and…he went around doing good and healing all who were under the power of the devil, because God was with him" (Ac 10:38).

But he is also a God who hates hypocrites: Jesus was scathing in his denunciation of the scribes and Pharisees (see Mt 23).

And he is a God who will 'spit' out of his mouth, those who are neither hot nor cold. (see Re 3:14-16).

Jesus warns us: It is not enough to accept him as our Saviour. We must go on to cultivate a relationship with him, by prayer, by learning his Word, listening to his voice, and by obeying his commands.

> "Not everyone who says to me, 'Lord, Lord' will enter the kingdom of heaven, <u>but only the one who does the will of my Father who is in heaven</u>. Many will say to me on that day, 'Lord, Lord, did we not prophesy in your name and in your name drive out demons and, in your name perform many miracles?' Then I will tell them plainly, 'I never knew you. Away from me, you evildoers!' (Mt 7:21-23).

The truth is that no one can accept Christ as Saviour sincerely and then continue to live without any change in their lifestyle.

> "Christ is either Lord of all, or he is not Lord at all" [9]

If we love him it will be our joy to keep his commands.

> "For we are God's handiwork, created in Christ Jesus to do good works, which God prepared in advance for us to do" (Ep 2:10).

Loving God with all your strength: Strength – capacity for exertion or endurance.

> "Be strong in the Lord and in his mighty power" (Ep 6:10).

---

[9] Hudson Taylor; Founder of the China Inland Mission.

Determine, decide with your will, to love God with all your strength. Not only with your moral strength but also with your spiritual strength. Strong in the power of the Lord who gives us the strength to love him with our whole being.

The Message Bible: This translation indicates a different slant on the commandment to love God with your whole being –

> Love the Lord your God with all your passion and prayer and intelligence. This is the most important, the first on any list. But there is a second to set alongside it: Love others as well as you love yourself. These two commands are pegs; everything in God's Law and the Prophets hangs from them" (Mt 22:37-40).

In other words, talk to God in prayer, using your emotions (heart) and your intelligence (mind).

Just as King David did in his powerful *Psalms*. He was a clever man and he always told God exactly how he felt. He understood that God knows how we feel anyway, so we may as well be honest when we come to him in prayer, asking for his help. Here are a few verses from *Psalm 69* where David cries out to God for rescue –

> "Save me, O God, for the waters have come up to my neck. I sink in the miry depths, where there is no foothold. I have come into the deep waters; the floods engulf me. I am worn out calling for help; my throat is parched. My eyes fail, looking for my God" (1-3).

The overlap: There is obviously some overlap between the heart, the soul and the mind.

> "The heart is the centre of a person's life, including the mind, will and emotions" [10]

But even if this is true, we know without a doubt that if we seek to love God with everything that is within us then we must –

- Keep our minds filled with his Word.
- Pray and listen for the voice of Jesus through his Holy Spirit.
- Get rid of any hindrances in our life.
- Obey him in all things.

We cannot afford to allow anything into our life that would stop us from loving him. only then will we be able to keep the first and most important commandment, to love the Lord our God with our whole being.

Loving others: If we do this then we will have no trouble keeping the second great commandment to love others as well as we love our self.

God's love, expressed in the Greek word *agape,* means having good will toward others, wanting the very best for them.

As we fill our heart and mind with the Word of God, we will display this good will toward others, wanting them to live a successful life and to forge good relationships. This is the same kind of life we want for ourselves.

Loving others will flow naturally from a heart full of love for God the Father, for Jesus the Son, and for the blessed Holy Spirit. The three in one!

---

[10] NIV Dictionary and Concordance.

As we guard our hearts from negative attitudes, and learn the principles taught by Jesus, and as we determine to follow him, seeking to love God with all that lies within us, we lay a solid foundation stone for a balanced Christian life.

Chapter Two:

Workers, Worshippers and Warriors

Under Moses the children of Israel were divided into various sections. There were the Levites, the workers who took care of the Tabernacle, the priests in charge of the worship and the warriors who were trained and prepared to protect Israel from any enemies.

For a balanced Christian life, we are to be workers, worshippers and warriors all in one package. Worship being the central balancing factor!

Without worship, praise and adoration, and the rich relationship this develops with God, we can fail to succeed as workers and warriors for him. But with that deep ongoing connection to our Lord we will live a victorious Christian life!

Working for God: The foundation of our work is built on four things:

- Our acceptance of salvation through Jesus' sacrificial death on Calvary.
- Our baptism in the Holy Spirit.
- Our careful study of God's Word
- Our obedience to his direction.

If we are in Christ then the tasks, we perform each day, even though they may be done for an earthly employer, are completed for God's glory. We should work faithfully, honestly, and ethically for our boss whoever he or she may be, knowing in our heart it is the Lord who is our ultimate employer.

As a lay person, the extra jobs we do for our church family should also be done cheerfully and with all diligence. Everything we do must be done as unto the Lord -

> "Whatever you do, whether in word or deed, do it all in the name of the Lord Jesus, giving thanks to God the Father through him" (Cl 3:17).

How can we best serve? The main task of every Christian is to find the will of God and then to work it out each day. Wisdom and direction for this can be found in his Word, but there are times we may need more specific directions, especially for those who are young and just starting out in life. Then there will be questions that need to be answered:

- What work does God want me to do?
- Am I going in the right direction?
- Am I studying the right things?

If you seek God's direction with your whole being, he will show you the way to go. The direction he wants you to take will become clear and peace will reign in your heart.

Over more than 70 years of Christian life the Lord has given me direction in different ways:

- Sometimes through a Bible verse.
- Sometimes in direct answer to my prayers.
- Sometimes through a counsellor.

Once I received direction through a non-Christian doctor and once through a child! God can use anyone. After all he spoke to Balaam through a donkey (see Nu 22:21-35).

However, you may be sure the direction God gives will always be in harmony with his Word.

At times God will speak through <u>a word</u> of personal prophecy. When this has occurred in my own life it has usually been confirmation of a scripture already impressed upon me. The personal prophecy has been an added assurance.

What is meant by a word? This is a modern expression, referring to a few words of comfort, encouragement, or exhortation, given by the Holy Spirit to the believer, or by one person to another. This can come in the form of a verse of scripture, or in ordinary conversational words, or by a prophetic revelation.

Be careful when receiving a personal prophecy that the person giving it is of good character and is someone you know you can trust.

When you have determined God's will, through the Word of God, through a counsellor, through a prophetic word or through a combination of all three, serve where he has placed you, using the abilities he has given you, and according to your gifts, temperament and personality.

How should we serve? Our work and service for God should be enthusiastic, joyful, and anointed by the Holy Spirit. The motive of our service for God should be pure and unselfish. It must be performed because of our love for God, not for gain or for praise of men.

If you will be content to do whatever God asks of you, however small, thus proving yourself to be a faithful worker, then he will give you other more challenging tasks. Just as children are trained to do more and more complex jobs as they mature so the Lord trusts us with more important work for him as we grow in wisdom and ability.

Do not sacrifice family: We should serve sacrificially too, though we should be careful it is ourselves we are placing on the altar, and not our family!

The ladder of life responsibilities should be clear for the lay person –

- God comes first in our life, with quiet times for prayer and the Word as we seek to know him better every day.

- We also need family recreation to keep ourselves and our dear ones healthy and happy, because our family are our first and foremost task given to us by the Lord.

- Then comes our job, as we must earn a living to support our family, along with quality time given to building healthy family relationships.

- After all these obligations, our work for the church comes last, though we should always be ready to serve the church as time and energy permit.

It is different for those who work full time in the Lord's work, for their job is inextricably linked to the church. For them the list of responsibility is God first, then family responsibilities, followed by their work in the church. If more pastors followed this order in their life, we would not have so many troubled spouses and children turning away from serving God because they feel neglected; their legitimate needs not being met.

God will bless your work: We do not all have to be pastors or leaders in the church. God has forever honoured other professions. Jesus himself championed honest work done with our hands. He did not think it beneath him to be a carpenter.

In Exodus 35: 30-35 God pours out his Spirit on the men who have the skills to build the Tabernacle -

> "Moses told the Israelites. 'See, God has selected Bezalel, son of Uri, son of Hur of the tribe of Judah. He's filled him with the Spirit of God, with skill, ability, and know-how for making all sorts of things, to design and work in gold, silver and bronze; to carve stones and set them; to

carve wood, working in every kind of skilled craft, and he's also made him a teacher; he and Oholiab, son of Ahasimach, of the tribe of Dan. He's gifted them with the know-how needed for carving, designing, weaving, and embroidering in blue, purple and scarlet fabrics and in fine linen. They can make anything and design anything.' (Message Bible).

So, ask God to bless the work you do, whatever it is, and he will be near to help you.

Jesus said in Matthew 11:30 - *"My yoke is easy, my burden is light."* When people get so caught up with working for God that they neglect their times of prayer and worship then trouble is not far away. That is because work for God, without refreshing times of worship and praise, can become hard, joyless and difficult!

Our worship: In 1 Chronicles 16: 29, in a Psalm of David we read –

> "Ascribe to the Lord the glory due his name; bring an offering and come before him. Worship the Lord in the splendour of his holiness."

And in John 4:23 Jesus said to the Samaritan woman –

> "Yet a time is coming and has now come when the true worshipers will worship the Father in the Spirit and in truth, for they are the kind of worshipers the Father seeks."

What is the definition of worship? It is reverence paid to God, or it can be an act of expressing reverence to God. It can also mean extravagant respect or admiration for, or devotion to, an object of esteem.

God gave his only Son and then Jesus offered himself for our salvation. In return he asks us to give ourselves to him, and to learn how to please him. (see Ro 12:1 & Ep 5:10).

Preparation for worship: We must prepare ourselves for worship otherwise it can become routine. We must display these attitudes of the mind and of the soul.

- **The attitude of reverence -**

"...I, by your great love, can come into your house; in reverence I bow down toward your holy temple" (Ps 5:7)

- **The attitude of humble penitence -**

"Have mercy on me, O God, according to your unfailing love; according to your great compassion blot out my transgressions. Wash away all my iniquity and cleanse me from my sin" (Ps 51:1-2)

- **The attitude of faith -**

"...Faith comes from hearing the message, and the message is heard through the word about Christ" (Ro 10:17).

The attitude of expectation: our expectation should be eager. What will God say to me today?

"He who searches our hearts knows the mind of the Spirit, because the Spirit intercedes for God's people in accordance with the will of God" (Ro 8:27).

Pure worship: This comes from hearts cleansed by the blood of Jesus and washed with the water of the Word. We should be repentant and humble, having spent time in meditation and preparation. Our worship then comes from a heart full of love and gratitude to Jesus for his wonderful sacrifice on the cross.

This is the balancing factor that ensures all the glory goes to God for anything we accomplish for him. Why is this? Because the Lord knows that our worship accomplishes three things for us –

Worship puts our life into perspective: In contrast to God's creative power as seen in the universe around us. We become aware that he is *God* -

"the blessed and only Ruler, the King of kings and Lord of lords, who alone is immortal and who lives in unapproachable light, whom no one has seen or can see" (1 Ti 6:15b-16).

In comparison we are as insignificant as a grain of sand, albeit only a little lower than the angels (see He 2:6-8).

Worship reminds us of his power and ability and so builds up our faith –

"Yours, LORD, is the greatness and the power and the glory and the majesty and the splendour, for everything in heaven and earth is yours. Yours, LORD, is the kingdom; you are exalted as head over all" (1 Ch 29:11).

Worship causes us to become increasingly aware of how loving and caring the Lord is and how much we need to depend on him –

"Cast all your anxiety on him because he cares for you" (1 Pe 5:7).

How do we worship? There are various areas in our Christian life and experience in which we are enabled to worship the Lord:

- **With our spirit:** Made alive by him; with our heart open to the truth of his Word –

"Therefore, if anyone is in Christ, the new creation has come. The old has gone, the new is here!" (2 Co 5:17).

- **With our mind:** Renewed by meditation on his Word –

"Therefore, I urge you, brothers and sisters, in view of God's mercy, to offer your bodies as a living sacrifice, holy and pleasing to God – this is your true and proper worship. Do not conform to the pattern of this world but be transformed by the renewing of your mind. Then you will be able to test and approve what God's will is – his good, pleasing and perfect will" (Ro 12:1-2).

- **With our body:** The temple of the Holy Spirit. What a privilege is ours: We are the temple of the living God –

"As God has said: 'I will live with them and walk among them, and I will be their God, and they will be my people' (2 Co 6:16b).

- **By our obedience to his will:** It is not true to say we love him if we are not obedient to his will revealed in his Word. It is not by what we say that God measures our love for him. It is by what we do, by our obedience to his will that he measures our love. We should seek to obey him in word and in deed: Jesus said to his disciples –

"If you love me, keep my commands" (Jn 14:15).

- **By our giving, both of our time and our money:** We do this when we spend time in serving him, and as we lay aside an appropriate amount each week for his work to be done efficiently and well –

"Each of you should give what you have decided in your heart to give, not reluctantly or under compulsion, for God loves a cheerful giver" (2 Co 9:7).

- **We worship also with our speech:** With words that issue from our heart in adoration and worship, describing our God, his love, his greatness, his goodness, and his mercy. As we read many times in the Psalms –

"I will give thanks to you, LORD, with all my heart; I will tell of all your wonderful deeds. I will be glad and rejoice in you; I will sing the praises of your name, O Most High" (Ps 9:1-2).

"I will extol the LORD at all times; his praise will always be on my lips. I will glory in the LORD; let the afflicted hear and rejoice. Glorify the LORD with me; let us exalt his name together" (34:1-2)

"For the Word of the LORD is right and true; he is faithful in all he does. The LORD loves righteousness and justice; the earth is full of his unfailing love". (33:4-5).

- **And we worship through singing –**

"Let the message of Christ dwell among you richly as you teach and admonish one another with all wisdom through psalms, hymns, and songs from the Spirit, singing to God with gratitude in your hearts" (Cl 3:16).

Our worship should also be sacrificial: God knows that even if we do not feel like praising him sometimes, when we do begin to worship, we are once again filled with joy as we dwell on his goodness; singing and making melody in our hearts -

"My sacrifice, O God, is a broken spirit; a broken and contrite heart you, God, will not despise" (Ps 51:17) "... Through Jesus, therefore; let us continually offer to God a sacrifice of praise – the fruit of lips that openly profess his name" (He 13:15).

Our worship should be fresh: We are commanded to praise the Lord, but not to say those same words "Praise the Lord" over and over, but rather to display in our worship fresh and vital truths about God.

Can I suggest this reverently? Is it possible in our Pentecostal churches that sometimes we weary God with our repetition? Other churches with their liturgies at least have a variety in their services. We charismatics, because we are determined to be spontaneous in our worship, can sometimes be repetitious and boring. We need to spend time thinking of new ways to praise and worship our Lord and Saviour.

When we are in a meeting it is too late to think of something new. Time must be spent before the Lord in a quiet place where we have precious moments to meditate on him and the wonders of his love, and all he has accomplished for us.

But you might say, "If I prepare beforehand my praise is not going to be anointed."

Is not the Holy Spirit with you in the secret place as well as he is in the assembly of his people? Yes, of course he is!

Therefore, sometimes we can be spontaneous and sometimes we can be prepared, but each time we can be anointed by the Holy Spirit. And the things God shows us in the secret place can have more depth and beauty, and more substance because we have had time to think and meditate on him and the wonders of his mighty love.

Worship using the truths of God, especially, those truths that will raise your faith and make God more real and powerful in your eyes. Such as:

- **He is present everywhere, he is omnipresent–**

    "Where can I go from your Spirit? Where can I flee from your presence? If I go up to the heavens, you are there; if I make my bed in the depths, you are there. If I rise on the wings of the dawn, if I settle on the far side of the sea, even there your hand will guide me, your right hand will hold me fast" (Ps 139:7-10).

- **He is all powerful, he is omnipotent –**

"To whom will you compare me? Or who is my equal? says the Holy One. Lift up your eyes and look to the heavens: Who created all these? He who brings out the starry host one by one and calls forth each of them by name. Because of his great power and mighty strength, not one of them is missing" (Is 40:25-26).

- **He knows all things. He is omniscient –**

"Do not tremble, do not be afraid. Did I not proclaim this and foretell it long ago? You are my witnesses. Is there any God besides me? No, there is no other Rock; I know not one" (Is 44:8).

- **He is the great Creator –**

"In the beginning God created the heavens and the earth" (Ge 1:1).

- **He loves us –**

"Satisfy us in the morning with your unfailing love, that we may sing for joy and be glad all our days" (Ps 90:14).

- **He planned our salvation before creation –**

"In him we were also chosen, having been predestined according to the plan of him who works out everything in conformity with the purpose of his will, in order that we, who were the first to put our hope in Christ, might be for the praise of his glory" (Ep 1:11-12).

- **He is our Sanctifier –**

"May God himself, the God of peace, sanctify you through and through. May your whole spirit, soul and body be kept blameless at the coming of our Lord Jesus Christ. The one who calls you is faithful, and he will do it" (1 Th 5:23-24).

- **And our exceeding great Reward –**

"And without faith it is impossible to please God, because anyone who comes to him must believe that he exists and that he rewards those who earnestly seek him" (He 11:6).

Worship using the Word: Here are some ideas for you!

Take a New Testament chapter each day and find in it all the things for which to thank and praise Jesus! This exercise will raise your faith and trust in God. Then, using what you have learned, write a Psalm. It is not too difficult. Here is a Psalm praising Jesus:

"Praise Jesus in the heavenlies,
Praise him at God's right hand,
Praise him for his power and glory,
Praise him for healing and miracles,
Praise him for free salvation,
Praise him for rivers of living water,
Praise him with tongues of men and angels,
Praise him for Holy Spirit baptism,
Praise him for our Counsellor who leads and guides us,
For all these things let us praise him,
Praise the Lord." *(AMC)*[11]

Worship using your gifts: We should all be seeking in every way to make our worship more spontaneous and more varied.

Here is a Psalm with an Australian flavour, written after the Queensland floods gradually flowed down to fill Lake Eyre in South Australia and turn it into an inland sea –

"The lonely stars shine in beauty,
singing serenely to God who created them from nothing.
The blazing sun rises to a new day,

---

[11] The poems marked *(AMC)* are written by the author of this book.

and in the distant horizon appears the circle of the earth.

"Far to the north clouds burst, dry creek beds run,
filled with swelling, sparkling, life-giving water.
Kangaroos and wallabies come to drink gratefully,
while desert flowers bend in the gentle breeze.

"Fish and frogs live again in the inland sea.
Eager birds follow, flying by your decree O Lord,
to feast royally.
Newly fledged birds praise God constantly
with joyous cacophony.

"Truly you are a good God,
you make the desert blossom as a rose,
even as you promised long ago.
You sustain life and care lovingly for your creation
in the lonely places.

"Your glory endures forever.
I will sing songs of the beauty of the Lord.
May my meditation be pleasing to him
in the night watches." *(AMC)*

Age is no barrier: Miriam must have been at least 86 when she followed her brothers Moses and Aaron through the Red sea. Yet she was dancing and singing and waving her timbrel, leading the women in praise and worship and extolling God's mighty power (see Ex 15:20-21).

So far, in this chapter we have established that our Worship must be the central balance to our Service. That worshiping our Lord, giving him praise and adoration, and building our relationship with him, gives us balance, otherwise our Work for God can be carried out in our own strength which saps our joy.

Our warfare: The foundation of our Warfare must also be worship. Indeed, worship, praise, and prayer must precede warfare for us to be built up and prepared to experience the victory Christ has won for us!

In addition to our "Work" and "Worship" our "Warfare" is important as another ingredient in a balanced Christian life. In Ephesians 6:10-12 we read about this warfare –

> "Be strong in the Lord and in his mighty power. Put on the full armour of God, so that you can take your stand against the devil's schemes. For our struggle is not against flesh and blood, but against the rulers, against the authorities, against the powers of this dark world and against the spiritual forces of evil in the heavenly realms".

Be warned: If we neglect our times of worship, our warfare can become weak and ineffectual instead of remaining strong and powerful.

What is spiritual warfare? How can we be useful to the kingdom of God in spiritual warfare? Warfare for God is not mysterious or hard to understand. It is simply making choices for the kingdom of God and then carrying out those choices.

Warfare is resisting temptation –

> "No temptation has overtaken you except what is common to mankind. And God is faithful; he will not let you be tempted beyond what you can bear. But when you are tempted, he will also provide a way out so that you can endure it" (1 Co 10:13).

Warfare is praying: Warfare is clothing yourself with the armour of God, but most of all it is praying in the Spirit –

"Stand firm then, with the belt of truth buckled around your waist, with the breastplate of righteousness in place, and with your feet fitted with the readiness that comes from the gospel of peace. In addition to all this, take up the shield of faith, with which you can extinguish all the flaming arrows of the evil one. Take the helmet of salvation and the sword of the Spirit, which is the word of God. And pray in the Spirit on all occasions with all kinds of prayers and requests. With this in mind, be alert and always keep on praying for all the Lord's people" (Ep 6:14-18).

Warfare is witnessing: Warfare is *evangelism*, telling others about Jesus and so increasing the population of the Kingdom of God. Jesus commanded us, "Go and make disciples of all nations" (Mt 28:19). It is telling our story to those who will listen, introducing others to Jesus Christ who loves them and has a plan for their life -

"How beautiful on the mountains are the feet of those who bring good news, who proclaim peace, who bring good tidings, who proclaim salvation, who say to Zion, Your God reigns!" (Is 52:7).

Warfare is healing: Warfare is helping, counselling, and healing those who need our message, our prayers, and our knowledge of the Kingdom of God and how it works. We follow in the steps of Jesus –

"God anointed Jesus of Nazareth with the Holy Spirit and power, and ...he went around doing good and healing all who were under the power of the devil, because God was with him" (Ac 10:38).

The need for warfare: The worst problems of the 21st Century seem to be anxiety and depression, leading to drug taking, drunkenness and other evils by those who do not know God. People everywhere are seeking peace, joy and satisfaction and God wants to bless them. God wants to increase his kingdom. Dare we keep him to ourselves? No, we cannot! God's love needs to flow through us into the lives of those who don't know him. If we will allow Jesus to shape us and train us for work in his kingdom and inspire us to worship him in spirit and in truth, then people will be drawn to us and through us to Christ.

Through our Work and our Warfare, empowered by our Worship, we will extend the Kingdom of God.

A true warrior: The Reverend Dr. Paul Ai: was born into a Buddhist family in Vietnam. As he grew into adulthood Buddhism did not satisfy him. Instead he became a witch Doctor worshipping 3,366 gods. After he attended a Christian meeting and discovered his gods were helpless in the presence of the one true God, he became a Christian. Over the next 25 years he spent 10½ years in prison because of persecution. He established churches in four of those prisons and brought hundreds of prisoners to Christ by his witness. Altogether he has started over 266 churches and in 1975 he became the General Superintendent of the Assemblies of God in Vietnam. You can read about his remarkable life in his book; *From Witchdoctor to Apostle*; *The amazing story of Jesus Christ's saving power in the life of Paul Ai.*[12]

A victorious Christian life becomes possible when we make sure to keep a careful balance between our work, our worship and our warfare.

---

[12] Published by Vision Outreach International; 1705 Todds Lane. Hampton VA. 23666 USA

Chapter Three:

How We Speak To God

It is very important to learn how to pray effectively for this brings an even balance and a firm foundation for our Christian life.

There are different methods of prayer: Each one of us must determine in our own heart how we will pray. The way we seek the Lord and bring him our requests may change over the years of our Christian life. Especially as we mature and learn more about other great leaders of the faith and their personal methods of prayer.

It is interesting to observe the way the Jews brought God into every compartment of their lives in Bible days. There was no separation between the secular and the sacred. Prayer was serious business and they believed in preparing for the prayer before speaking to the Lord. In Ecclesiastes we are warned to be careful of our words -

> "Do not be quick with your mouth, do not be hasty in your heart to utter anything before God. God is in heaven and you are on earth, so let your words be few" (Ec 5:2).

We need to be free of sin: The Lord will not hear those who have allowed the negative effects of sin to dominate their life -

> "Surely the arm of the Lord is not too short to save, nor his ear too dull to hear. But your iniquities have separated you from your God; your sins have hidden his face from you, so that he will not hear" (Is 59:1-2).

We need to free our mind: Daily empty your mind of unhealthy thoughts, mistakes, errors, and criticisms. First learn from them, then put them out of your mind. It takes time, but the mind learns to obey!

> "If you allow dark thoughts, regrets, resentments and the like to accumulate, your whole psychology can in time be so adversely affected that a major effort may be required to bring it back to a normal state of balance." [13]

Instead we should concentrate on Paul's word to the Philippians –

> "Forgetting what is behind and straining toward what is ahead, I press on toward the goal to win the prize for which God has called me heavenward in Christ Jesus" (Ph 3:13b-14).

Our attitude to prayer: There are many things to consider before we begin to pray. Some, who have had loving parents have no trouble seeing God as a loving Father, others who have been abused by their earthly parents may find this difficult. They need deep healing of sad and terrible memories before they can see God as a caring heavenly Father who loves unconditionally.

Other Christians who have seen many answers to prayer have no trouble viewing God as Almighty, able to perform miracles. By searching his Word, they see God as one who keeps his promises, one who will move to protect them from evil and bring them safely into his eternal kingdom.

No matter how we perceive God, one thing is needful: we must see the answer to our prayer complete in the heavenly realm by faith, before it can come to pass here on earth.

> "I will give you the keys of the kingdom of heaven; whatever you bind on earth will be bound in heaven, and

---

[13] *Enthusiasm Makes the Difference* by Norman Vincent Peale. Page 30

whatever you loose on earth will be loosed in heaven" (Mt 16:19).

"Dear friends, if our hearts do not condemn us, we have confidence before God and receive from him anything we ask, because we keep his commands and do what pleases him" (1 Jn 3:21).

Gratitude is important: Have an attitude of gratitude for answered prayer and for God's rich blessings toward you. It is good to keep note of the requests you make to the Lord, for how can you be thankful for the prayers that are answered if you have not kept account? The Apostle Paul asks us in Philippians to make our requests with thanksgiving. -

"Do not be anxious about anything, but in every situation, by prayer and petition, **with thanksgiving**, present your requests to God" (Ph 4:6).

There are many blessings the Lord gives to us daily. Compare your life to the life of someone in a refugee camp and you will soon realise you have much to thank God for each day of your life.

Have we taken our luxuries of clean water, decent food and safe shelter for granted? Have we been ungrateful children, and do we need to ask forgiveness for this ingratitude?

Prayer is a serious business: We cannot pray before we have thought carefully about our needs and the needs of others for whom we want to pray.

Do we believe God will answer our prayer? Is our faith strong? Do we know for sure we are praying within the parameters of his will?

We must pray from the heart, sincerely, if we want God to listen. Think carefully before you pray, then you can rest in the assurance that God will give your prayer serious consideration.

There is something else to think about. Will the answer to your prayer cost you something? Will it bring about a difference in your own life? Will God see you need to change in some way before he can answer your prayer?

Martin Luther (1499-1552) was instrumental for the beginning of the Protestant Reformation when he nailed his Ninety-Five Theses to the door of the Church at Wittenberg, Germany. He used to pray for two hours each day, but any day he was extra busy he prayed for three hours. From this we can see why he was such a catalyst for change and why he was able to bring freedom to those who listened to him preach.

Luther's suggestions on prayer:

"It is a good thing to let prayer be the first business of the morning and the last at night. Guard yourself carefully against those false, deluding ideas which tell you, 'Wait a little while. I will pray in an hour; first I must attend to this or that.' Such thoughts get you away from prayer into other affairs to hold your attention and involve you so that nothing comes of prayer for that day.

"In a sense everything a believer does is part of his/her worship and prayer to the Lord but if we break the habit of true prayer then in the end we will become lax and lazy, cool and listless toward prayer and our enemy is not lazy or careless".[14]

So, start the day with a quiet time with the Lord, reading and meditating on scripture and then asking him to guide you through the day. Pray for those you love and commit them to God's protection. Pray for those in government and for world leaders that God's will be done, and his plans carried out.

---

[14] Quotes from *A Simple Way to Pray* written in 1535 by Martin Luther.

Meditation: When you have completed your prayer, it is time to wait on God for him to speak to you. As you review your day the Lord may point out changes you need to make in your life, so your prayer can be answered, or he may show you a need to change your prayer in some way. He may bless you with a wonderful revelation from his Word or he may guide you in a new direction. It is good to keep note of these thoughts so you can look back to see how the Lord has led you in the past.

This is one thing I regret, not keeping note over the years of all the answers to prayer, small and large. No matter how good your memory, you will miss much of the richness of what the Lord wants you to keep as a memorial of his doings in your life if you do not keep note.

Praying using scripture: Choose appropriate scriptures to cover what you want to pray about then weave them into your prayer. In this way you are praying in God's will, using his words, saying back to him what he has promised you in his Word -

> "Praying Scripture filled with God's promises is a powerful prayer principle. God's Word is his will and by praying what he says in his Word, you are confidently submitting your will to God who knows all things." [15]

Jesus taught us to pray –

> "Our Father in heaven, hallowed be your name, your kingdom come, your will be done, on earth as it is in heaven. Give us today our daily bread. And forgive us our debts, as we have also forgiven our debtors. And lead us not into temptation but deliver us from the evil one" (Mt 6:8-13).

---

[15] *Prayers That Avail Much* by Germaine Copeland. Page 3

- Using the Lord's prayer as a template we could pray for the will of God to be done.
- For our daily bread, physical and spiritual.
- For a forgiving spirit,
- and for deliverance from evil satanic attacks.

Always remembering that the Kingdom belongs to God and he is in control to carry out his purposes in earth and in heaven.

Our prayers should be suited to the Kingdom of God: They should be bold and persistent, reflecting God's mercy, grace and benevolence.

Bold prayers: God is more willing to give than we are to receive but he waits for us to come to him in faith, believing that he will answer us. Remember our prayers must be prayers of faith and not of presumption. That means we cannot pray outside of the will of God. However, he will always answer our believing prayer, though he may say "no" or "later".

What can we pray for, apart from our personal needs and the needs of our loved ones? We can pray for revival, for souls to be swept into the kingdom. We can pray for God's healing power to be manifest, declaring to the world that our God is able. We can pray for God's will to be done on earth as it is in heaven -

> "Ask and it will be given to you; seek and you will find; knock and the door will be opened to you. For everyone who asks receives; the one who seeks finds; and to the one who knocks, the door will be opened" (Lu 11:9-10).

Persistent prayers: When we have decided what we want from the Lord we should **ask** and keep on asking. Meanwhile we should **seek** to know his will in the matter. Having laid out our foundation for our prayer, and believing we are praying within the parameters of the will of God, then we should **knock**. This indicates a door to be opened to bring about the answer to our prayer. When we reach this goal, we move into a new level of answered prayer.

Prayers that reflect God's love: When we pray it should be with the understanding that God loves us dearly and that he is willing to answer us. That his arms are open and stretched out to pour blessings upon us, his dear children.

Some Christians pray short prayers constantly throughout the day, others spend specific time alone with God, some are intercessors, who will continue to pray until they feel the answer is obtained. Others pray using the Word. There are many ways that we can pray. The important point is that we are persistent in our prayers.

There is another form of prayer: A special prayer of agreement to be prayed together with one or two other people for a specific reason.

- First pray carefully in your first language.
- Then pray in other tongues so the Holy Spirit can share the burden of your petition.
- When you feel the burden lift then thank God together in faith for the answer.
- Do this on a regular basis, perhaps on one day each week, until the answer comes.

Prayers of Bible characters: They extoll the might and power of the Lord; confess on their own or their nations behalf, and finally make their needs known.

Hannah's prayer: (1 Sa Ch. 2). This woman of God had just dedicated her son Samuel to serve the Lord as she had promised. She prays exultantly, as she is brimming over with a sense of accomplishment, of obedience and fulfillment.

God had answered her prayer and given her a son to serve him for life -

> "There is no one holy like the Lord; there is no one beside you; there is no Rock like our God" (vs. 2).

She goes on to contrast God's power to bless his people with his judgment on those who follow wickedness -

> "The Lord brings death and makes alive; he brings down to the grave and raises up. The Lord sends poverty and wealth; he humbles, and he exalts. He raises the poor from the dust and lifts the needy from the ash heap; he seats them with princes and has them inherit a throne of honour" (vs. 6-8).

She continues exalting in the power of God and concludes with a prophecy -

> "He will give strength to his king and exalt the horn of his anointed" (vs. 10b)

Daniel's prayer: (Daniel 9:1-19). He realises that seventy years have passed for the prophecy of Jeremiah to be fulfilled, the promise that God would forgive his people and reinstate them in their land after seventy years. Here is that promise from Jeremiah-

> "This is what the Lord says: When seventy years are completed for Babylon, I will come to you and fulfill my good promise to bring you back to this place" (Je 29:10).

Daniel begins his prayer with praise and worship, acknowledging God's righteousness and the gross sin of the nation -

> "I prayed to the LORD my God and confessed: Lord, the great and awesome God, who keeps his covenant of love with those who love him and keep his commandments, we have sinned and done wrong. We have been wicked

and have rebelled; we have turned away from your commands and laws" (Da 9:4-5).

He continues in this way until finally he challenges God and gives him a reason why he should keep his promise -

> "Give ear, our God, and hear, open your eyes and see the desolation of the city that bears your Name. We do not make requests of you because we are righteous, but because of your great mercy.
>
> Lord, listen! Lord, forgive! Lord, hear and act!
>
> For your sake, my God, do not delay, Because, your city and your people bear your Name" (vs. 18-19).

This prayer of Daniel's is a great template for anyone who is praying and interceding for their nation. In the New Testament we are encouraged, indeed commanded, to pray for those who rule over us (see 1Tim 2:1-4).

Background to Paul's prayer: The Apostle Paul first gives the foundation of his prayer for the Ephesians -

He tells them of the mystery, hidden until then, that the Gentiles were to be blessed along with Israel. Together they were to form the church through the Holy Spirit -

> "This mystery is that through the gospel the Gentiles are heirs together with Israel, members together of one body, and sharers together in the promise in Christ Jesus" (Ep 3:6).

After affirming his position as God's servant, he goes on to tell them they can pray freely because, through God's eternal purpose, Jesus has made the way open -

> "In him and through faith in him we may approach God in freedom and confidence" (vs. 12).

Paul's prayer: He prays for the wonderful things Jesus has won for them to be manifest in their lives, such as strength and power, possible through faith -

> "I pray that out of his glorious riches he may strengthen you with power through his Spirit in your inner being, so that Christ may dwell in your hearts through faith" (vs. 16-17a).

He goes on to describe just how wonderful the love of God is, and his description reminds us of the Holy of Holies which was also a cube, equally wide, long, high and deep which contained the Mercy Seat. Paul knows if they are rooted and grounded in love, then they will be able to grasp how much God loves them -

> "And I pray that you, being rooted and established in love, may have power, together with all the Lord's holy people, to grasp how wide and long and high and deep is the love of Christ, and to know this love that surpasses knowledge – that you may be filled to the measure of all the fullness of God" (vs. 17b-19).

He finishes with superlative praise to our God who can do all things -

> "Now to him who is able to do immeasurably more than all we ask or imagine, according to his power that is at work within us, to him be glory in the church and in Christ Jesus throughout all generations, for ever and ever! Amen" (vs. 20-21).

Personalise this prayer: We can take this prayer to ourselves, accepting the same blessings that Paul prayed for the Ephesians. We are sharers together in the same strength and power and love, and we too can go on, by faith, to believe that the power of God is at work in us to do far more than we can possibly imagine.

Jesus' teaching on prayer: As Philip Yancey reminds us in his book on prayer:

> "Jesus taught a model prayer, the Lord's prayer, but otherwise gave few rules. His teaching revolves down to three general principles. Keep it simple. Keep it honest. Keep it up! Mainly Jesus pressed home that we come as beloved children to a Father who loves us in advance and cares deeply about our lives." [16]

As we continue to learn to pray and receive answers to our prayers our Christian life is strengthened and balanced even more strongly.

---

[16] *Prayer-Does it Make a Difference* by Philip Yancey. Page 183

Chapter Four:

How God Speaks To Us

To live a balanced Christian life, we also need to know, and listen to, the voice of our Saviour, through the blessed Holy Spirit he poured out after his resurrection.

He promised his disciples -

> "If you love me, keep my commands. And I will ask the Father, and he will give you another advocate to help you and be with you forever – the Spirit of truth. The world cannot accept him, because it neither sees him nor knows him. But you know him, for he lives with you and will be in you. I will not leave you as orphans; I will come to you" (Jn 14:15-18).

Jesus gave this strong promise to the disciples who were filled with apprehension at the thought of him leaving them alone without his constant loving fellowship and strong leadership. Remember they were not then filled with the Holy Spirit and power. This experience would later give them the courage and boldness they needed to do his will.

During his ministry here on earth Jesus often used ordinary scenes to illustrate his teachings, and here is one to help us to recognise his voice.

The illustration of the shepherd -

> "Very truly I tell you, anyone who does not enter the sheep pen by the gate, but climbs in by some other way, is a thief and a robber. The one who enters by the gate is the shepherd of the sheep. The gatekeeper opens the gate for him, and the sheep listen to his voice. He calls his own sheep by name and leads them out. When he has brought

out all his own, he goes on ahead of them, and his sheep follow him because they know his voice" (Jn 10:1-4).

In Bible days shepherds mingled their flocks at night for safety reasons. In the morning, when it was time for the shepherds to separate their flocks, it was a simple matter of the shepherds standing at widely different points and calling their sheep. The sheep, hearing their shepherd's voice, went to him willingly, trusting him to provide fresh pastures, quiet waters, healing for hurts and safety from predators.

You can see this scene acted out in some middle eastern countries even today.

How can we be sure we know the voice of Jesus? Is the voice just our imagination? How can we tell? Here are some of the things I have learned over the years:

- The voice of Jesus leads us gently, he does not nag or condemn.
- His voice will always agree with the revealed Word of God found in the Bible.
- He is consistent, he does not change his mind from day to day.
- God will confirm the word he has given us through some other means if we ask him.

Remember though, God is not normally in a hurry, he sees ahead, so don't rush in if you are not sure he is speaking to you. If you are unsure, and especially if you do not have peace in your heart, then it is best not to do anything.

However, if on the other hand you feel God is asking you to do something that is not contrary to his Word, and is something that will bring blessing to someone, without hurting anyone else, then go ahead. God will be pleased that you were obedient to what you thought might be his leading.

You will learn gradually as you are obedient: one step at a time; remaining sensitive; looking for these things:

- Agreement with the Word of God.
- Good counsel from someone you trust.
- Peace in your heart.
- Confirmation.

Through the written Word: As a young mother with little ones to care for I was distressed that I could not share in my husband's ministry until God reassured me from a verse in Scripture that I would share one day in his reward. Years later I was given this same verse again from a ministry I trusted so the message was confirmed to me once more.

The verse given to me comes from Samuel and it concerns David's troops who were quarrelling over who should share in the booty their army had just won. Some soldiers had been left to guard the baggage, along with the stuff they had already gathered. The rest were instructed to go on fighting to complete their victory over the enemy. Those who had fought did not want to share with those who had been left behind to guard the camp. David made a wise decision: -

> "The share of the man who stayed with the supplies is to be the same as that of him who went down to the battle. All will share alike" (1 Sa 30:24).

God can speak to us in many ways, sometimes he gives direction through his written Word, sometimes with light for our future. This happened to me in Tasmania where we had pastored for 16 years -

One morning as part of my Scripture for the day I read Genesis 28:15 –

> "I am with you and will watch over you wherever you go, and I will bring you back to this land. I will not leave you until I have done what I promised you."

These were words spoken by God to Jacob, while he was on his long journey from his home into an unknown future, but I felt strongly that there was a message there for us.

Two days later my husband, Ken, received an invitation from Alan Langstaff to join Vision Ministries in Sydney. I remembered the verse in Genesis when I heard of the invite and was able to share it with Ken. I had no doubt that God had made this verse stand out to me for a good reason.

Since then God has kept the promise that he showed me that day in Genesis and has watched over us through many journeys. We left Tasmania, spent two years in Sydney then ten years in the USA. Now we are back in Sydney and have journeyed back to Tasmania for ministry many times.

I believe that the world-wide ministry the Lord has given us of taking the *Whole Word to the Whole World* through Vision Colleges is part of what he promised us. This is still ongoing with thousands of students in over a hundred countries around the world graduating from our colleges and going on to plant many churches.

Be aware though, if you are seeking a word from God; it is not right to indulge in spiritual roulette. That is, opening the Bible at random, and reading any verse you happen to see first.

God can use what you have memorised: What you put into your mind God can use; so, learn appropriate scripture verses, then the Holy Spirit can remind you of the one you need when you are searching for guidance. Jesus promises us that the Holy Spirit will teach us and remind us of scriptures we have memorised (see Jn 14:26).

This happened to me one time in the USA where we spent the ten years from 1980-1990. Ken was very ill, and the doctor was not sure if he had gallstones or cancer or an aneurism. I was full of fear wondering how I would manage in a strange country with three children, but without my husband.

One morning that week I woke up with the last verse of Psalm 91 going through my mind, "With long life I will satisfy him and show him my salvation". Immediately my fears vanished, I was filled with faith and knew everything would be alright. My faith was rewarded as Ken was prayed for and completely healed overnight. This was proved by an Xray; much to the doctor's astonishment.

Because I knew this verse in Psalm 91 God was able to use it to speak to me for Ken's healing and this inspired my faith!

If you know the Word of God and have memorised helpful scriptures then you will be able to minister life to others, using an appropriate verse God brings to your mind.

I have known two ministries that have used this method of using the Word of God. One was an American pastor, Dick Mills, who has since gone to be with the Lord, and the other is my husband's brother, Dr. Barry Chant. For this ministry various persons are chosen from the congregation and given two or three scriptures and a few words of encouragement. This is very effective, and people respond well, as it is the Word they are hearing. Using this method requires learning many scriptures and being able to recall them, and their place in the Bible, so it is not for everyone. Then too, there must be prayer, preparation and the anointing of the Holy Spirit on the minister himself for the word to be effective.

Through his still small voice –

> "The Lord said, 'Go out and stand on the mountain in the presence of the LORD, for the LORD is about to pass by'. Then a great and powerful wind tore the mountains apart and shattered the rocks before the LORD, but the LORD was not in the wind. After the wind there was an earthquake, but the Lord was not in the earthquake. After

the earthquake came a fire, but the Lord was not in the fire. And after the fire came a gentle whisper. When Elijah heard it, he pulled his cloak over his face and went out and stood at the mouth of the cave. Then a voice said to him, 'What are you doing here, Elijah' " (1 Kg 19:11-13).

Elijah's experience must have been terrifying, but God did not speak through the earthquake, the wind or the fire. He spoke softly to Elijah, giving him a new commission and promising him a partner in ministry. This was Elisha, who would be a help to Elijah in his ministry and later succeed him as prophet (see vs. 14-18).

Jesus also leads gently: "There is now no condemnation for those who are in Christ Jesus" (Ro 8:1). It is instead Satan who nags and condemns the Christian.

The Holy Spirit will always be consistent: What he says will agree with the already revealed Word of God. If you need a word of direction, then resist soulish thoughts in the name of Jesus and then ask him to speak to you. Wait on him, do not rush. Have a note-book handy to write down anything that comes to your mind, then you can read it later to help you in deciding what God wants.

What is meant by <u>a word</u>? As explained in chapter two, this is a modern expression, referring to a few words of comfort, encouragement, or exhortation, given by the Holy Spirit to the believer, or by one person to another, which can come in the form of a verse of scripture, or in ordinary conversational words.

Be aware too of the hypnopompic state, that state between sleeping and waking when your mind is clear. God can speak to you in that moment. This has happened to me twice. Once when Ken was deathly ill and then another time when I was about to hear that my father had passed away. This second time I woke with Psalm 23:4 going through my mind: "Yea, though I walk through the valley of the shadow of death, I will fear no evil; for You are with me; Your rod and Your staff, they comfort me" (Ps 24:4 NKJV) This verse was quickened to me and I thought perhaps God wanted me to preach on it. I walked over to my desk to make a note of it and as I did the phone rang. It was my sister Barbara to tell me about my father's death. We were still in the USA when this happened, and I felt very sad to be apart from my family at such a time. However, I was also filled with wonder that God had been so good in preparing me for the news. That he even knew where I was and that I was about to receive the phone call.

As it was impossible for me to get to the funeral in time my family understood I could not come. Then another wonderful thing happened. About a year before his death I had been moved to write a prayer and send it to my father, one I would have prayed over him if I could have been with him in person. He thanked me at the time but without my knowing he instructed that this prayer was to be read at his funeral. So, though I could not be there in person, I had a voice there in spirit. God is so good. Sometimes it is only in looking back that we can see God's guiding hand was there all the time.

Through an audible voice: -

> "The Lord came and stood there, calling as at the other times, 'Samuel! Samuel' Then Samuel said, 'Speak, for your servant is listening' (1 Sa 3:10).

We should not seek to hear an audible voice. God is sovereign and he will speak if he sees fit. There are testimonies of people who have heard an audible voice which turned them toward God.

We constantly hear these days of Muslims who are hearing God speak to them. God is good and he is giving them a chance to understand who Jesus is through dreams and visions. Stuart Robinson has written a book on this subject; *Mosques and Miracles: Revealing Islam and God's Grace.* [17]

Through an angel: Balaam was on his way to prophesy over the children of Israel when his donkey blocked his way for the third time -

> "When the donkey saw the angel of the LORD, it lay down under Balaam, and he was angry and beat it with his staff. Then the LORD opened the donkey's mouth, and it said to Balaam, 'What have I done to you to make you beat me these three times' (Nu 22:27-28).

Balaam's eyes were opened to see the angel of the Lord with a flaming sword who was barring his way. He was permitted to continue his journey but with strict instructions to speak only the word given to him by the Lord.

Angels do figure in many Old Testament stories, however we should not seek to speak with angels, though they are God's messengers. If we do seek angelic visitations this can open the way for Satan to deceive us. Angels spoke frequently in Bible days, and even today people have been warned and helped by someone, not realizing until they had gone that it must have been an angel.

Through a vision: -

> "At Caesarea there was a man named Cornelius, a centurion in what was known as the Italian Regiment. He and all his family were devout and God fearing; he gave generously to those in need and prayed to God regularly. One day at about three in the afternoon he had a vision. He distinctly saw an angel of God, who came to him and said, 'Cornelius!' Cornelius stared at him in fear. 'What is it, Lord?' he asked. The angel answered, 'Your prayers

---

[17] *Mosques and Miracles* by Stuart Robinson, CHI Books; P.O. Box 6462, Mt. Gravatt, Brisbane QLD. Australia

and gifts to the poor have come up as a memorial offering before God' (Ac 10:1-4).

Cornelius was devout, generous, feared God and prayed on a regular basis but he was not expecting a vision. This was a visitation from the Lord and Cornelius was amazed and fearful at the sight of the angel who told him that God was aware of his prayers and gifts to the poor.

As with Cornelius, be aware that God is watching what we do and taking note, as Malachi tells us: -

> "Then those who feared the LORD talked with each other, and the LORD listened and heard. A scroll of remembrance was written in his presence concerning those who feared the LORD and honoured his name" (Mal 3:16-17).

About the same time Cornelius was seeing his vision in Caesarea the Apostle Peter was praying in Joppa while waiting for his lunch. Peter was not looking, or asking for a vision either, but God gave him a strange vision which he later realised concerned Cornelius. (see Ac 10:9-48).

If God wants to give a vision to someone, he will give it. If not, no amount of praying, begging or seeking will bring a vision. If we persist, we are more likely to be deceived by Satan who is always seeking whom he may devour (see 1 Pe 5:8).

Through these visions God was able to bring Peter and Cornelius together so that Cornelius and his household could hear the good news about Jesus and receive the baptism of the Holy Spirit. Peter rejoiced, realising God was showing him the wonderful truth that the Gentiles were to receive salvation as well as the Jews.

Through dreams: In Genesis Joseph had dreams and he also interpreted dreams. Much later Daniel interpreted dreams for Nebuchadnezzar. There were not many with this ability. This was obviously a God-given gift, given to devout and pure servants of God. Nowadays some are endeavouring to return to interpreting dreams with varied results.

I have been a Christian for more than 70 years but can only remember two personal dreams I have had that later proved accurate. If Jesus speaks to you through a dream you will know it and will not forget it, though you may not realise the significance of it until many years later.

Christians do not need another person to give them a word from God, though this can happen as a confirmation of something God has already told them. Mature Christians can ask God for a word for themselves. Be cautious, if you do receive a word from someone be careful to confirm any directional prophecy by seeking counsel from someone you trust.

The Shepherding Movement: During our ten years in the USA a cult sprang up that gave people direction for their life, such as when to sell their house or car, or when to move to a different State, and this caused terrible disruption in families. Sometimes it was the husband and sometimes the wife who believed in the directions given but sometimes their spouse refused to agree. Some marriages ended in divorce causing much sadness, until the pastors giving these directions were rebuked by the wider church and they realised their error.[18]

What was forgotten by these men were the words of Peter that we are all priests before God, and we can go to him personally for any guidance we need. We should allow no one to speak direction into our life unless either it is a confirmation of what God has already revealed to us, or we

---

[18] *The Shepherding Movement* by David Moore. https://www.goodreads.com/The Shepherding Movement.

later receive confirmation from another source we can trust (see 1 Pe: 2:4-5).

I remember another sad case where a visiting preacher in a Sydney church gave a word to a young lady that her father had sexually abused her when she was young. She had no recollection of this but believed what she had been told and consequently accused her father. He maintained his innocence and the rest of the family sided with him. The young lady became estranged from her family. What a tragedy. People who give words like this should realise the devastation they may cause. The young lady should have discussed the situation with her pastor who surely would have advised her to wait for confirmation of such a serious word.

Psychic New Age experiences: What about psychic phenomena? In my book *Healing – the Wonder and the Mystery* I used a quote which I will repeat here as it is so important. It is from Joanna Michaelsen, who came from a psychic background, where people claim to know the future. She became a committed Christian and has this advice to give -

> "People with psychic gifts who become Christians should wait twelve months and learn the Word of God very well before using God's spiritual gifts."[19]

Remember this, if we aren't walking in the truth, with a clear conscience, we will not hear from God no matter how much we ask; but when everything is in place and God does speak to us, we will not forget what he has said.

Through circumstances: Sometimes God closes doors, sometimes he opens doors, at other times he asks us to wait.

---

[19] Ministries Magazine Spring 1985; pp.69

In *The Sound Of Music,* the film that has been voted the most popular ever made, one of the actors says,

> "When God closes a door, sometimes he opens a window."

This is true. God can move in many ways. We need to remember that he knows best.

Make sure you are right with God, resist Satan and then, if the circumstances remain, thank God for his guidance. It is natural to wonder sometimes, when we are going through puzzling times, if we really are going in the right direction. It is only later, as we look back on our life, we can see God was leading us after all.

Through spouse or children: Sometimes God speaks through a spouse or through children within the family circle. Make sure your spouse is walking in the Spirit. Husbands particularly have the final decision on any matter, so their responsibility is great. If you cannot agree, pray together and then ask God to lead.

Does God speak through the children in a family? In my experience I would say sometimes he does! Out of the mouths of babes...!

Through a friend: Sometimes even through a stranger! Be careful. Look at their life, see the fruit, is it good? If so, then you can trust their words will be beneficial (see Mt: 7:16).

God speaks to us in many ways. He can speak to us in our prayer times if we remain quiet before him and spend some time listening for his voice. For this we need to shut out all the business of this modern era. Such as the television, radio and mobile phone.

During perilous times: At times God's guidance and direction become more strongly apparent, especially during times of great trouble, war or persecution.

Be assured if God needs a task performed, he will somehow make it clear. If we are not listening, he will speak to some other person. One way or another God will arrange for his will to be done.

Learning to listen for the voice of the Holy Spirit and then obeying him carefully is another good foundation stone for a balanced Christian life.

Chapter Five:

Champions / Overcomers

There are many great heroes and heroines of the faith who have overcome difficult circumstances and completed exploits for God, because they made certain to lead a life of balance and maturity.

A champion: "One who wins first place, one who shows marked superiority."

An overcomer: "One who surmounts difficulties and attains superiority."

Here are two remarkably similar definitions that we can explore. What is true of the one can also be true of the other.[20]

Jesus is our ultimate champion. He gained salvation for us, so that we also could become champions and overcomers. He said to his disciples -

> "In this world you will have trouble. But take heart! I have overcome the world" (Jn 16:33b).

In the Bible we see many who overcame. Here are a few of them.

Joshua became leader of Israel after Moses death and he believed God's Word to him –

> "Keep this Book of the Law always on your lips; meditate on it day and night, so that you may be careful to do everything written in it. Then you will be prosperous and

---

[20] Webster's Dictionary

successful. Have I not commanded you? Be strong and courageous. Do not be afraid; do not be discouraged, for the Lord your God will be with you wherever you go" (Js 1:8-9).

Gideon was slowly transformed from a coward to a brave champion as he obeyed each command of God -

"When the angel of the Lord appeared to Gideon, he said, 'The Lord is with you, mighty warrior' (Jg 6:12).

Paul the apostle suffered many things. He was flogged, imprisoned, shipwrecked and stoned. He was exposed to death and attacks by bandits many times, but he never allowed himself to become a victim. He was always a champion for God who told him -

"My grace is sufficient for you, for my power is made perfect in weakness.' 'Therefore,' (said Paul), 'I will boast all the more gladly about my weaknesses, so that Christ's power may rest on me. That is why, for Christ's sake, I delight in weaknesses, in insults, in hardships, in persecutions, in difficulties. For when I am weak, then I am strong' (2 Co 12:9-10).

Mary the mother of Jesus obeyed the Lord and trusted him with her life when she agreed to bear Jesus our Saviour. She sang, -

"For the Mighty One has done great things for me - holy is his name. His mercy extends to those who fear him, from generation to generation" (Lu 1:49-59).

Hannah was the wife of Elkanah: The Lord heard her prayer for a child and granted it. She gave birth to Samuel and then kept her promise to give him to the Lord. She was filled with thanksgiving. -

"There is no one holy like the Lord; there is no one besides you; there is no Rock like our God" (1 Sa 2:2).

Esther became a queen. She was only a young girl, but she delivered her people from a terrible danger. Her uncle Mordecai encouraged her -

"Who knows but that you have come to your royal position for such a time as this" (Es 4: 14b).

In history also there are many champions/overcomers. Many great men and women of God have spent their lives in his service, overcoming great obstacles along the way.[21]

Charles T. Studd (1862-1931) was a missionary pioneer. He was converted under Moody and Sankey and he dedicated his life and his inherited fortune to the Lord. He then spent nine years in missionary service in *The China Inland Mission* before he had to leave because of ill health. Years later he served for six years as pastor of the Union church at Ootacamund, South India, then worked toward opening Africa from the Nile to the Niger for missions.

David Brainerd (1718-1747) was a missionary to the American Indians. He baptised 85 Indians of whom half were adults. He had to relinquish his mission because of tuberculosis. He bore hardship and suffering with heroic devotion and died at the age of only 29 years. Brainerd kept a diary of his life and work among the Indians. This diary was published by Jonathan Edwards as *Brainerd's Journal*.

William Booth (1829-1912) was founder and first General of the Salvation Army. He organised the army under military form, name and discipline, to bring the message of salvation to the poor and destitute. The movement was first named, *East London Christian Revival Society*. He lived to see his organisation spread into fifty-five different countries. He travelled about five million miles and preached nearly

---

[21] *The Wycliffe Biographical Dictionary of the Church*, by Moyer S. Elgin.

60,000 sermons. Booth wrote a book, *In Darkest England and the Way Out.*

Katharina Von Bora (1499-1552) was Luther's wife. She was a feisty woman who once removed Luther's office door after he shut her out. She would hide their valuables as Luther was so generous that he was constantly giving their things away. It was a happy marriage and she bore Luther three sons and three daughters. She also looked after the scholars who boarded with their family and bought a farm in order to feed them all. Luther called her the Morning Star as she arose so early each morning.

Mary Slessor (1848-1915) was a missionary to West Africa. She was born in Aberdeen, Scotland and after working with youth in the Dundee slums she sailed for Nigeria in 1876. She served first in the Okoyong area and then at Itu among the Ibo people. She fought against witchcraft, drunkenness, twin-killing, and other cruel customs. She had an unusual combination of qualities, humour and seriousness, roughness and tenderness, vision and practicality. She was a powerful influence for Christianity in the region. She was instrumental in establishing the *Hope Waddell Institution* to train Africans in useful trades and to carry out medical work.

Mother Teresa (1910-1997) was a missionary to the poor and destitute. She saw the untouchables of India dying in the streets and had compassion on them and she inspired many other women to join her in her ministry of mercy. During a war in Lebanon she prayed for the guns to stop firing at a certain time, to give her opportunity to rescue many children and bring them out of the war zone. The guns stopped, at the time she had requested the Lord, enabling her ambulances to travel safely through the dangerous streets to reach the children. [22]

My husband had an opportunity to meet Mother Teresa, when he was asked by her to give a series of talks in San Diego, to raise money for a hospice she was planning to build in Mexico. His description of her at that time was -

> "A great woman, small in stature, but with an indomitable will. It is no wonder she was able to accomplish so much."

The rewards for overcomers: Overcomers are promised many wonderful rewards when they arrive at the gates of heaven (Re 2:7-3:21).

- They will have the right to eat from the tree of life.
- They will have a victor's crown.
- They will not be hurt by the second death.
- They will be given the hidden manna, a new name.
- They will have authority over the nations and will be given the morning star.
- Their names will never be blotted out of the book of life
- They will be a pillar in the temple of God.
- They will have the right to sit with Jesus on his throne.

These rewards are figurative in nature and we cannot imagine exactly what the apostle John saw in our future, but we do know that we will have eternity to praise and glorify our Lord.

---

[22] *Mother Teresa, The Early Years* by David Porter

Natural and spiritual: What is true in the natural dimension can also be true in the spiritual sphere as the Apostle Paul declares -

> "Forgetting what is behind and straining toward what is ahead, I press on toward the goal to win the prize for which God has called me heavenward in Christ Jesus" (Ph 3:13b-14).

What are the natural goals of champions/overcomers, and what spiritual truths can we learn from them?

Champions dream of winning: -

> "They see themselves holding the gold medal."

As Christians, we can also use our imagination to see ourselves as God's champions, becoming overcomers through the power of the Holy Spirit he has poured out on us, and wearing the crown of life he has promised us. Joel prophesied long ago of the outpouring of the Holy Spirit we are seeing today -

> "And afterward, I will pour out my Spirit on all people. Your sons and daughters will prophesy, your old men will dream dreams, your young men will see visions" (Jl 2:28).

Some psychologists maintain this truth: They tell us that if you can see yourself doing something in your imagination then it is possible for you to accomplish it.

The psychologist, Alfred Adler (1870-1937) would direct his clients to do tasks that would change their beliefs, feelings and habits. He assigned roles for his clients AS IF they were successful, AS IF they were courageous, AS IF they were happy, and so on, with great success.[23]

---

[23] *Baker Encyclopedia of Psychology & Counseling* by David Benner & Peter Hill

Psychologist William James also claimed this "AS IF" principle. He said, "If you want a quality, act as if you already have it. Try the "AS IF" technique. It is packed with power and it works."

It would not be right however to act AS IF you had the money to pay your bills when in fact you do not. We must always be honest in all our dealings.

John Wesley, the founder of Methodism, was terrified during a journey by a storm at sea. He noted that other Christians on board were calm and asked them how they could be so serene. Their answer was that they had faith in God's loving care, and they taught him to act AS IF he had faith during the storm. To discipline himself to act AS IF he had courage, to act AS IF he was calm and assured. Wesley followed their advice and developed a strong faith that helped him through many difficult times.[24]

The way this system functions is threefold and, though it is psychology of a sort, the idea can be used by any Christian with the help of the Holy Spirit. If you are fearful and want to develop courageous faith, then imagine you have that faith already. Then, act AS IF you already have bold faith. Ask yourself this question. What would I do now if I had strong faith? This will depend on your circumstances at the time. Finally, keep on believing that you have faith and that, with the Lord's help, you will continue to show strong faith where before you were fearful.

I learned this AS IF principle after I developed a fear of long plane flights to the USA. The Holy Spirit brought to my mind something I had learned about horse riding. When you are riding a horse and you come to a high jump, the idea is to "throw your heart over". In other words, imagine yourself

---

[24] *Enthusiasm Makes the Difference* by Norman Vincent Peale pp.25-26

already on the other side of the jump, landed safely. This is what I realised I must do by faith. I had to imagine AS IF I had already landed in the USA before the plane had even taken off from Sydney airport. This faith stance took away all my fear of flying.

People with anxiety and depression can be helped to overcome these afflictions in time through counselling, being taught to trust in God, changing the way they think, and controlling their trigger thoughts, those sad thoughts that lead on to other equally distressing thoughts.

It is amazing what the human brain is capable of. Marvellous discoveries can be made in science, simply by thinking about the universe and experimenting in the laboratory.

Disabilities can be overcome by training the brain to make up the deficiency suffered from a stroke or catastrophic accident. Through various exercises the retrained brain simply uses different brain cells to do the work formerly done by the part that has been damaged or destroyed.

Medical science is only now beginning to understand the complexities of the brain. For twenty years Professor Colleen Loo has been leading research on a low frequency electric stimulation that can help the brain to reorganise and lift depressive symptoms. Professor Loo says -

> "What we are doing is very slightly shifting the electrical resting potential of the nerve cells...changing the likelihood of whether they will fire or not".[25]

God knows how amazing our brains are, since he created them, and so, as he observed the men building the tower of Babel he said -

---

[25] Sydney Morning Herald; April 23rd.2019; *DIY Brain Zap Brings Help to the Bush.*

> "If as one people speaking the same language; they have begun to do this, then nothing they plan to do will be impossible for them" (Ge 11:6).

Using our imagination: If we can see ourselves doing something for God, then we should strive to fulfil this faith vision, through education and learning, and through prayer and practise.

Billy Graham described how he first learned preaching skills. He would go out into the woods and preach to the trees, learning his craft slowly but surely. He became one of the greatest preachers of all time and in his lifetime preached successfully to more people than any other man in history. He recently went home to be with the Lord at 99 years of age.

Champions have a fire within them: -

> "Athletes have mountains of enthusiasm to bring to the job of winning."

We Christians have been granted this same excitement for our task by the Lord Jesus who promised -

> "You will receive power when the Holy Spirit comes on you; and you will be my witnesses" (Ac 1:8a).

The Greek word for power is *dunamis,* from which we get our word dynamite. Not unused and unlit dynamite but dynamite that is exploding, showing its tremendous power. With the baptism in the Holy Spirit promised to us, we gain the power and enthusiasm we need to attract others to Christ.

If you want to get people's attention, then pray for miracles of healing. People are attracted to power and when they see God's power working, bringing healing, they are more ready to receive Jesus as their Saviour.

Champions are not defeated by defeat:

> "Even when a particular athlete fails in his first attempt, if he is championship material he won't stop trying, he will go on to try, try, try again."

As Christians we should not cease to serve the Lord, even if at times we fail him by allowing sin into our life. If this happens, we should repent quickly and then go on working for the Lord with our eyes fixed on Jesus, trusting him to cleanse and forgive us. He has promised through the apostle John that –

> "If we confess our sins, he is faithful and just and will forgive us our sins and purify us from all unrighteousness" (1 Jn 1:9).

Our worst defeat was the death of our second son Gavin James. He was born with complications and died after living for only two days. That experience was heart breaking but through it came a determination to believe God for more children even against medical advice. Over time God gave us courage and the certainty of victory and eventually he gave us a daughter and two more sons to complete our family. The story is told in detail in my book *Divine Healing, The Wonder and the Mystery*.[26]

Why is it we have valley experiences, times of seeming failure and sorrow? Because without the valleys where we learn and grow in Christian character, there would be no contrasting mountain tops of victory. In Isaiah God promises us strength and refreshing even in the valleys -

> "The poor and needy search for water, but there is none; their tongues are parched with thirst. But I the Lord will answer them; I the God of Israel, will not forsake them. I will make rivers flow on barren heights, and springs

---

[26] Vision Publishing.2006

within the valleys. I will turn the desert into pools of water, and the parched ground into springs" (Is 41:17-18).

The emotionally poor and needy search for relief and God can help them if they will learn about him and his faithfulness. There are so many needy people depressed by the terrible things that are happening in the world. We need to learn to strengthen our trust in God and cast our burdens onto his shoulders. The apostle Peter had personal experience of the love of Jesus, who forgave him after he denied him three times, and he tells us: -

"Cast all your anxiety on him for he cares for you" (1 Pe 5:7).

Hannah Hurnard learned to overcome fear and anxiety by turning them into opportunities for faith.

"The sooner fear is got rid of and turned into faith the better. I learned this as a very young Christian through reading a little article in a C.W.A.G. magazine; an article written for nervous, worried and anxious people. It said something like this: 'never mind if temperamentally you are very fearful and prone to anxieties and worries, for that gives you a wonderful opportunity to practice more faith than other people. Turn every fear into faith and at once, look what an advantage you have! Endless opportunities of putting God's gracious promises to the test and of trusting him.' This new, lovely idea gripped my heart and gave me a completely new attitude towards. my fears. They could all be turned into faith. It seemed to me that this gave me almost an unfair advantage over normal, healthy people. For people who have more opportunities than others for practicing faith ought surely to be able to develop a strong faith more quickly than others." [27]

Champions set their sights high: -

> "Second or third place is not what a champion aims for, no, he strains every effort to be the winner and to take the reward."

As Christians we also need to keep our eyes fixed on the highest place, where God dwells with Jesus seated at his right hand. We should strive to gain the heavenly inheritance promised to us -

> "Since, then, you have been raised with Christ, set your hearts on things above, where Christ is, seated at the right hand of God. Set your minds on things above, not on earthly things" (Cl 3:1-2).

By keeping a faith vision of future victory, we can look forward to becoming an overcomer indeed. Heaven should be more real to us than the things we see with our natural eyes. If we can keep this heavenly vision, then it will be easier to believe for answers to prayer. Here is a meditation on heaven, written after the death of a loved one -

> As heaven is where Jesus is, Jesus is where heaven is!
> Because Jesus is closer than a brother,
> with us to the end of the age
> and dwelling in us through his Holy Spirit,
> Heaven is closer than we think!
>
> Because we are earth bound, we cannot see
> the glories of heaven with our eyes; nor hear its beautiful music
> with our ears, but they are there none the less.
> God is there with Jesus, and his mighty angels,

---

[27] *Hearing Heart* by Hannah Hurnard; Page 47

and the saints who have served him victoriously.

If God was to open our eyes to see and our ears to hear
we would be amazed at the glory surrounding us!
Because of this our loved ones who have gone to sleep in Jesus
are closer than we can imagine.
There is only a veil between.

We can look forward to being able to see them because
Heaven is more real than this world of ours.
Earth's mountains, and seas, and abundant trees and flowers
are ephemeral and insubstantial by comparison.
A vapour that will one day pass away.

Heaven is real and true, more solid than things we see
with our eyes and touch with these hands of ours.
Its music is more wonderful than any we hear on earth.
Jesus our Saviour is heaven's glorious King and he has
promised to prepare a place for us there.

As we grow older, we dream of heaven
and of walking and talking with Jesus.
Even though we may be a small and humble part of his plan,
we know he will have time for us,
because he is present everywhere,
and available to anyone who needs him.

Heaven feels very near when our loved ones go before us.
They will stand with Jesus at heaven's gate
to greet us when we come.
We don't know how they will appear,
but we will know them instantly
as they wait to welcome us into heaven's glory.
There we will be together forever. Amen! *(AMC)*

Champions anticipate problems: -

> "Athletes do not forget important points but look ahead to see what will assist them in reaching their goal."

We Christians also should look ahead to make sure we do not make occasions for stumbling by our own lack of foresight. Like the scouts we should, "Be Prepared". We can guard against temptation by looking ahead and avoiding dangerous moments. Then God will do his part. (see 1 Co 10:13)

We must put on the whole armour of God so that we can take our stand against the devil's schemes (Ep 6:11), and keep a balance of work, worship and leisure as discussed in Chapter two of this book. This balance should come from our relationship with Jesus. If we follow this path, then our work for God will be easy and joyful.

Champions refuse to give up: -

> "Champions continue on year after year, practising, exercising, keeping their bodies in shape, striving ever onward toward the prize they seek."

We too should keep on, striving after the prize of the high calling for which we have been predestined (see Ph 3:13-14) -

> "Because the sovereign Lord helps me; I will not be disgraced. Therefore, have I set my face like flint, and I know I will not be put to shame" (Is 50:7).

Here is one of those pre-incarnation glimpses concerning Jesus as he set himself courageously to face the cross to complete our redemption.

I have always been overawed by the courage of Jesus because he must have seen many thousands crucified during his lifetime. When he was only eleven years of age a man, Judas the Galilean and his followers fought against Rome. He attacked the Royal Armory in Sepphoris, only four miles from Nazareth where Jesus lived. The vengeance of Rome was swift and terrible. They burned down Sepphoris and took many citizens to become slaves. Then they crucified 2,000 of the rebels along the roadsides as a warning. [28]

Jesus saw this and knew the agonies of crucifixion, yet bravely went ahead with his ministry knowing what lay ahead. He was determined to complete the will of his Father, knowing that his sacrifice would bring about our salvation.

In his steps: We should follow in the steps of Jesus, determining to continue our Christian walk no matter what trials we face -

> "Therefore, my dear brothers and sisters, stand firm. Let nothing move you. Always give yourselves fully to the work of the Lord, because you know that your labour in the Lord is not in vain" (1 Co 15:58).

The robbery we suffered while moving from Minnesota to San Diego to begin a Bible College was one trial that could have defeated us. That day we lost all the worldly goods stacked in our moving van. All the materials needed for the Bible College were in that van. What were we to do?

Instead of collapsing in despair my husband Ken prayed through to a place of surrender. The books he had written we knew we could regain as there were copies in Australia, but he had lost so much; forty years of study notes, lecture notes, sermons prepared, and many wonderful insights given him by the Lord. Thoughts that he might never be able to regain.

After his prayer of surrender, and his promise to the Lord to begin again to rewrite his sermons and seek for more revelation from the Lord, the phone rang to say the moving van had been discovered. God restored Ken's books, sermons, lecture notes and student records. They were all

---

[28] William Barclay's Commentary of N.T. Luke 9; *The Conditions of Service.*

discovered safe within the van. Everything else was gone to various flea markets in other states so there was no hope of recovery.

Fortunately, we had some insurance. This replaced about a third of our belongings, but we were woefully under insured compared to the replacement costs. Many Christian friends, both in Australia and in the USA helped us with gifts of money, and some local church members gave us second-hand furniture, so despite our trials we were blessed abundantly.

Had we given up and returned to Australia then we would have missed meeting Dr. Stan DeKoven who has been instrumental in spreading our Vision Colleges around the world. Sometimes it is only in looking back we can see the guiding directing hand of the Lord leading us in the right path to complete his will.

Champions visualise themselves as champions: -

"They see in their imagination the task already completed, and the prize already won."

We too must see ourselves as overcomers in Christ. We are new creations, the beginning of a new race -

"Praise be to the God and Father of our Lord Jesus Christ, who has blessed us in the heavenly realms with every spiritual blessing in Christ. For he chose us in him before the creation of the world to be holy and blameless in his sight. In love he predestined us for adoption to sonship through Jesus Christ, in accordance with his pleasure and will" (Ep 1:3-5).

"See what great love the Father has lavished on us, that we should be called children of God! And that is what we are! The reason the world does not know us is that it did not know him. Dear friends, now we are children of God, and what we will be has not yet been made known. But we know that when Christ appears, we shall be like him, for we shall see him as he is" (1 Jn 3:1-2).

As Leo Harris, founder of *CRC Churches International* taught us, "Jesus is the beginning of this new race. In his glorified body he transcended space and time but could still sit and eat with his disciples. There is a glorified man up there in heaven!" [29]

Champions seize opportunities: -

"Wherever there is opportunity to practise or to compete champions will be there; nothing but injury or illness can stop them from the desire to compete which consumes them."

As Christians we should always be ready to do what is required, while we have strength of soul and body, we should endeavour to complete the will of God for our life.

Our work is to do good to everyone, especially to our brothers and sisters in Christ. Our witness is to those who don't know Jesus and his saving power. We can witness by our life and by our deeds as well as by our words -

"Therefore, as we have opportunity, let us do good to all people, especially to those who belong to the family of believers" (Ga 6:10).

Our conversation, when we are witnessing, should be gracious and kind, as we seek to bring others into the kingdom -

"Be wise in the way you act toward outsiders; make the most of every opportunity. Let your conversation be always full of grace, seasoned with salt, so that you may know how to answer every man" (Cl 4:5).

---

[29] From a sermon preached in CRC Churches Int. Sturt St. Adelaide circa 1950

If we invite someone to a meal then the words, "seasoned with salt" represent a meal of friendship. In Middle Eastern culture having a meal together was proof of trust between friends. We must be ready to witness whenever opportunity arises, but our witnessing must be seasoned with friendship, not rushing in to give our testimony without getting to know the person first. This will prove we really care about them.

Jane Van Opstal, a missionary in Cambodia illustrates this idea. She makes friends with children using puppets. She teaches them hygiene and explains how important it is for them to wear shoes in their climate where worms can enter through the bare feet and cause much illness. The children love her and bring their mothers to hear her. In turn the mothers bring the fathers and so a church is born. Jane has been instrumental in the founding of over fifty churches and she has taught others her methods and so expanded her ministry. [30]

Here again are the eight attitudes toward becoming champions/overcomers for God.

- We must dream of winning
- We must have the fire of enthusiasm within us
- We must not be defeated by defeat
- We must set our sights high
- We must anticipate problems
- We must refuse to give up
- We must visualise ourselves as champions
- We must seize every opportunity[31]

"In all these things we are more than conquerors through him who loved us" (Ro 8:37).

---

[30] Christianity Today; August 2000

[31] The quotes of the characteristics of the champion were found in a Reader's Digest article, *Secrets of Olympic Heroes* by Jeff Bond, Registered sport and exercise psychologist.

It is through learning how to be overcomers in our Christian life that we lay a further foundation stone for balance.

Chapter Six:

Encouragement

To live a balanced Christian life, we must learn how to encourage ourselves and each other in the Lord. Seeking his guidance and direction to overcome all difficulties. In this chapter David shows the way from defeat to victory.

David's experience: -

> "David was greatly distressed because the men were talking of stoning him; each one was bitter in spirit because of his sons and daughters. But David found strength in the LORD his God" (1 Sa 30:6).

At this time David has plunged from the heights of popularity, as the son-in law of King Saul, into the depths of despair as an outlaw leader who is facing rebellion among his troops. How did this come about?

During the years when David was escaping from king Saul's murderous intent to kill him, he spent time assisting the Philistines in some of their battles. On this occasion David had led forth his soldiers, as mercenaries, to battle alongside Achish, a Philistine commander, but Achish decided not to use David and his men at this time. Instead he sent them back to their homes in Ziglag. There, to their horror, they found that an enemy had attacked and taken, not only their goods, but their wives and children as well.

His soldiers blamed David as their leader because he had neglected to leave anyone to guard the village while they were away. They were so distraught they were prepared to stone him in revenge.

David's response was to strengthen and encourage himself in the Lord. He knew if he did so then God would find a way to replace everything and everyone lost to them.

Training for kingship: God used this occasion, as well as other times of trouble, to complete David's training for kingship.

Initially, David had been given the task of moulding 400 men, who had come to him in debt, discouraged, and discontented, into a fighting army. He had performed this admirably thus proving his leadership ability. Now he faced a rebellion among the men he had trained.

David's secret: In this present terrible time of trouble David had a lot to discourage him, but instead he built up his courage.

Psalm 143:1-5 shows us David's secret. One he used many times -

> "LORD, hear my prayer, listen to my cry for mercy; in your faithfulness and righteousness come to my relief. Do not bring your servant into judgment, for no one living is righteous before you. The enemy pursues me, he crushes me to the ground; he makes me dwell in the darkness like those long dead. So my spirit grows faint within me; my heart within me is dismayed. <u>I remember the days of long ago; I meditate on all your works and consider what your hands have done.</u>"

In that psalm David, in his misery, remembered God's mighty deeds and meditated on them. He recalled what he had been taught about the Exodus and all God had done for his ancestors. He thought on those triumphant days when God had proved his power, challenging and overcoming all the Egyptian gods, making a way through the Red Sea for the children of Israel, and drowning the Egyptian army who pursued them (See Ex chs.1-15).

There was one more thing David could do to encourage himself. He could recall his anointing by the prophet Samuel and keep a faith vision of one day being crowned king of Israel (see 1 Sa 16:1-13).

Our own Christian experience: We too can go from a mountain top of blessing into a valley of testing. However, if we have the right attitude during our spiritual battles we can mature into strong warriors for God. If we are willing and obedient, he will use the testing times to grow and develop our Christian character.

We should learn from David not to give up, but to keep going by encouraging ourselves in the Lord.

How should we encourage ourselves when we are feeling a failure - down, depressed, and sorrowful? We should follow David's example and meditate on God's mighty works.

But we have so much more to remember than David did!

We have the Old Testament, of which David had only a part, and we have the New Testament as well, depicting the many miracles wrought by Jesus and the apostles. The greatest miracle of all was the resurrection of Jesus from the dead, which is the measure in this dispensation of the Almighty Power of God!

There is even more given to us: See the blessings promised in just the first two chapters of Ephesians:

- We are saints,
- Grace and peace are ours,
- We have been blessed with every blessing,
- We were chosen before the foundation of the world,
- We are predestined,
- We have been adopted into God's family,
- We are redeemed,

- We are forgiven,
- God's grace is lavished on us,
- Wisdom and understanding are ours,
- God's will is made known to us,
- We have been included in Christ,
- We have been sealed with the Holy Spirit,
- We have a guaranteed inheritance,
- We are called to hope,
- We have a glorious inheritance,
- God's incomparable great power is in us,
- God has given us life,
- We are seated in heavenly places,
- We are saved by grace,
- We are God's workmanship,
- We have been brought near through Christ's blood,
- We have been reconciled with others,
- We have access to the Father,
- We are fellow citizens with God's people.[32]

Surely these are more than enough to raise our faith and thankfulness and encourage us to believe for great things.

There is still more to remember: We also have the miracles performed by historical figures to contemplate.

One of these miracles involved St. Benedict of Nursia and the iron head. St Benedict was a monk (480-543 AD) who established his own monastery as he thought other monasteries were not disciplined enough. His rules were strict.

His organisation:

- At the head of each monastery was an Abbot.

---

[32] A more complete list can be found in *Living in the Image of God* by Barry Chant. Page 35

- His monks took the vows of poverty, chastity, and obedience to a superior.
- Days were divided into exercise, manual labour and educational instruction, accompanied by worship, meditation and study.
- Simplicity was encouraged in every aspect of life.

These four rules became the foundation for all monastic establishments. [33]

Here is the miracle of the iron head:

"At another time, a certain Goth, poor of spirit, that gave over the world, was received by the man of God; whom on a day he commanded to take a bill, and to cleanse a certain plot of ground from briers, for the making of a garden, which ground was by the side of a lake. The Goth as he was there labouring, by chance the head of the bill slipped off, and fell into the water, which was so deep, that there was no hope ever to get it again. The poor Goth, in great fear, ran to Maurus and told him what he had lost, confessing his own fault and negligence: Maurus forthwith went to the servant of God, giving him to understand thereof, who came immediately to the lake: and took the handle out of the Goth's hand, and put it into the water, and the iron head by and by ascended from the bottom and entered again into the handle of the bill, which he delivered to the Goth, saying: "Behold here is thy bill again, work on, and be sad no more." [34]

We can read in 2 Kings 6:1-10 of a similar miracle wrought by Elisha.

---

[33] The Wycliffe Biographical Dictionary of the Church; by Elgin S. Moyer; Page 38
[34] Book two of the Dialogues: *Life of St. Benedict* ch.6 by St Gregory the Great. (540-604).

Miracles in the 20th century: If these marvels are not enough, we also have the twentieth century with the outpouring of the Holy Spirit and the many great ministries raised up by God to inspire our faith.

Miracles are still happening in the twenty first century and the greatest miracle of all is the baptism of the Holy Spirit with signs following. Because of this we should keep a faith vision of the "heavenlies" where Paul tells us, we are seated with Christ -

> "Since, then, you have been raised with Christ, set your hearts on things above, where Christ is, seated at the right hand of God. Set your mind on things above, not on earthly things" (Cl 3:1-2

David's first step to victory: First, as we have seen, David encouraged himself in the Lord and built up his courage by remembering past miracles and blessings.

His second step: David enquired of the Lord -

> "Then David said to Abiathar the priest, the son of Ahimelek, 'Bring me the ephod'. Abiathar brought it to him, and David enquired of the Lord, 'Shall I pursue this raiding party? Will I overtake them?' 'Pursue them' he answered. 'You will certainly overtake them and succeed in the rescue' (1 Sa 30:7-8).

How did he enquire of the Lord?

David had Abiathar, the son of Ahimelek the High Priest, with him and because Abiathar had the Ephod, David was able to enquire of the Lord and determine his will by using it.

What was the Ephod?

The Ephod was a breastplate worn by the High Priest which included a pocket containing the Urim and Thummim.[35]

What were the Urim and Thummim?

According to C. W. Slemming: These were one black stone and one white stone secreted in the breastplate of the High Priest. The person needing to know the will of God would ask a question and then the High Priest would reach in and draw out a stone. The white stone indicated a positive answer and the black stone gave a negative answer. These stones enabled persons to enquire of the Lord.

No one knows for sure exactly what the Urim and Thummim were and as they were not very reliable, they soon vanished from Israel's history. At this moment in time however, David was able to seek the will of God with some success.

How did Abiathar come to be with David?

King Saul had ordered the slaughter of Ahimelek, the High Priest, and the other priests with him after they gave assistance to David and his soldiers. They had fed them with Temple bread when they were fainting and hungry, thus giving help to Saul's enemy, David. Abiathar was the only priest who escaped, and he sought refuge with David's army. (see 1 Sa 22:9-23).

Because of this David was able to ask Abiathar, who was now High Priest, to bring out the Ephod so he could enquire what to do. Abiathar drew out the white stone indicating a positive answer which he gave to David.

The Lord has a way of arranging our lives. So that direction is available when it is needed. However, unlike David we do not need the Ephod or the Urim and Thummim. We can go straight to the throne of God to pray for guidance, and we

---

[35] These Are the Garments by C. W. Slemmimg ch.22

can also search the Word of God to assist us in determining his will. We are instructed by James:

> "If any of you lacks wisdom, you should ask God, who gives generously to all without finding fault, and it will be given you" (Ja 1:5).

His third step: David received help along the way from a slave. An unexpected source! (see 1 Sa 30:11- 16).

In verse fifteen we read: -

> "David asked him, (the slave they had captured) 'Can you lead me down to this raiding party?' He answered, 'Swear to me before God that you will not kill me or hand me over to my master, and I will take you down to them.'

With the help of this Egyptian slave David was able to find his enemy and overcome him.

David was open to receive help and information, and we can also look for extra help during our times of testing if we need it. Perhaps from friends and family, a counsellor or even a stranger. God is able to arrange for someone to help us when we need it.

His fourth step: David marched forward to victory, regaining all that was lost to the army (see 1 Sa 30: 16-20).

We can also follow these four steps in times of discouragement and gain victory in our life.

Our own steps to victory: Don't give up, do what David did.

- Encourage yourself in the Lord by remembering the miracles of the past.
- Seek the Lord's direction and make your requests known to him.
- Be watching for God to help you through someone, or in some way.

- Go on to victory trusting in God's faithfulness to keep you safe in him.

"Don't fret or worry. Instead of worrying, pray. Let petitions and praises shape your worries into prayers, letting God know your concerns. Before you know it a sense of God's wholeness, everything coming together for good, will come and settle you down. It's wonderful what happens when Christ displaces worry at the centre of your life" (Ph 4:6; The Message Bible).

Confidence: If you can follow these steps, they will help you to develop a good healthy self-image. You will have confidence in yourself and your ability to do God's will, and you will be able to say -

"I can do all things through Christ who strengthens me" (Ph 4:13).

David's decree: (see 1 Sa 30: 21-25).

After the battle David made a decree that those who stay to guard the baggage get the same reward as those who go on to gain the victory -

"The share of the man who stayed with the supplies is to be the same as that of him who went down to the battle. All will share alike" (vs.24).

God's decree: For some of us it is God's decree that we stay at home taking care of the mundane and the ordinary. Those who are not called to public ministry can pray and seek the Lord for those who are, the pastors, the missionaries and the evangelists.

We are not all called to the fiercest battles of life, but we are all to be rewarded in the end if we are faithful. So, encourage yourself, by looking back with rejoicing for past blessings, keeping a faith vision of the "heavenlies" where you are seated with Christ. Then pray with thanksgiving, looking forward in faith and go on to victory, regaining any lost ground in Jesus Name!

The victory we gain in Christ, through strengthening and encouraging ourselves, and each other, and through following his direction, is one more precious foundation stone for a balanced Christian life.

Chapter Seven:

Jesus Cares for You

For a balanced Christian life, we must believe without wavering that we are loved and cherished by the Lord who is love.

The compassion of Jesus: During his earthly ministry Jesus showed his love and care for the poor, the sick, the hungry and the despairing and after his resurrection Jesus continued to show his loving care, especially toward his disciples.

When Mary Magdalene met him in the garden on the morning of his resurrection, he asked her, "Woman why are you crying. Who is it you are looking for?" (Jn 20:15). When he spoke her name, "*Mary,*" and she realised who he was, she was overjoyed to see him. So much so that he had to restrain her enthusiasm: "Do not hold onto me, for I have not yet ascended to the Father" (20:17a).

It moves me deeply to know that Jesus paused in this most important journey to his heavenly Father because he heard Mary crying and took pity on her.

Then he gave her a message for the disciples. What a privilege for Mary, to announce the stupendous news that Jesus was alive from the dead!

Jesus also showed his compassion to Peter, who was suffering agonies of remorse for having denied his master three times. He had wept bitterly, thinking Jesus would not trust him anymore. But instead Jesus lovingly made him reverse his denials with three positives. "Do you love me?"

And then gave him instructions to feed the lambs and take care of the sheep (see Jn 21:15-17).

He had forgiveness for Thomas, with no rebuke, as he showed him his hands and side. Of course, Thomas was overwhelmed and breathed, "My Lord and my God'" (20:28).

However, Jesus did point out to Thomas that those who believed without seeing would be more blessed than he. Jesus was referring to those of us who would believe down through the ages of the Christian era. (see 20:24-29).

Jesus cares about you: -

> "Cast all your anxieties on him for he cares for you" (1 Pe 5:7).

Jesus proved his care for us by his willingness to suffer on the cross.

These days many people feel inadequate and insignificant, so worthless, helpless and inferior that it cripples their life. Some feel constantly put down and negated by government, by banks, by bosses, and by people who bully them.

Some feel they are just a number on a passport or a credit card, and they are only measured by their ability to produce or consume.

Jesus came to show us a different story, he came to show us that God loves us extravagantly -

> "See what great love the Father has lavished on us, that we should be called children of God" (1 Jn 3:1a).

We can have complete confidence in God because we know he cares. Because of his great love we can have confidence that life will make us stronger; that it will not break us. We learn to cast our burden on the Lord because we know he will sustain us; he will never permit us to be moved -

> "Cast your cares on the LORD and he will sustain you; he will never let the righteous be shaken" (Ps 55:22).

Then we can accept each experience, not passively, but with vibrant, positive faith in God who will help us to overcome by his Word, because we know that God arranges our life so that everything works out eventually for good as Paul tells us in Romans -

> "We know that in all things God works for the good of those who love him, who have been called according to his purpose" (Ro 8:28).

Jesus cares enough to forgive: Our God who is willing to forgive our sin, is also the God who will forgive because he loves us, as we read in Psalm 103:11-12 -

> "For as high as the heavens are above the earth, so great is his love for those who fear him; as far as the east is from the west, so far has he removed our transgressions from us."

If you have repented of your sins and accepted Jesus as your Saviour, he has forgiven you. Leave the burden of your past with him, do not look back, but look instead to the future -

> "Forget the former things; do not dwell on the past. See, I am doing a new thing! Now it springs up; do you not perceive it? I am making a way in the wilderness and streams in the wasteland. The wild animals honour me, the jackals and the owls, because I provide water in the wilderness and streams in the wasteland, to give drink to my people, my chosen, the people I formed for myself that they may proclaim my praise" (Is 43:18-21).

Jesus cares about your deliverance from sin: Because you are born again God has taken away your stony heart and given you a new heart of flesh. He has replaced your old sin nature with his nature. He has promised us a new heart and a new spirit (see Ez 36:26) -

> "Therefore, there is now no condemnation for those who are in Christ Jesus, because through Christ Jesus the law of the Spirit who gives life has set you free from the law of sin and death" (Ro 8:1-2).

It is no use trying, by yourself, to get rid of sin or any other bondage. What you need to do is to cling to the person of Jesus, then all the things that bother you will fall away.

> "Nothing in my hand I bring. Simply to thy cross I cling" [36]

Thomas Chalmers (1780-1847) preached a sermon with the title, *The Expulsive Power of a New Affection.* [37] The idea is that we become so in love with Jesus that we are happy to turn away from sin. Here is a quote from his sermon -

> "We know of no other way by which to keep the love of the world out of our heart, than to keep in our hearts the love of God—and no other way by which to keep our hearts in the love of God, than building ourselves up on our most holy faith."

But, for this to happen, we must want Jesus with all our heart, and we must mean business with God like the psalmist of long ago -

> "As a deer pants for streams of water, so my soul pants for you, my God. My soul thirsts for God, for the living God. When can I go and meet with God?" (Ps 42:1-2).

If we fix our eyes on Jesus, he will transform us through the washing of the Word of God. We can't transform ourselves. It is a psychological fact that the more we try the worse we get, because concentrating on the problem of sin emphasizes it

---

[36] Quote from *Rock of Ages* by A. M. Toplady; Redemption Hymnal
[37] Dr. Thomas Chalmers First Moderator of the Free Church of Scotland 1843

more in our mind. The best way to avoid sin is to replace it with good thoughts and good actions.

Here is a quote from William Barclay which explains this perfectly.

> "The loveliest garden I ever saw was so full of flowers that there was scarcely any room for a weed to grow. In no garden is it enough to root up weeds, flowers must be sown and planted until the space which the weeds would have usurped is filled. Nowhere is this truer than in the world of thought and thoughts. Often, we are troubled by wrong thoughts. If we go no further than to say to ourselves. "I must not think about that; I will not think about that," all that we are doing is fixing our thoughts on it more and more. The cure is to think of something else, to banish the evil thought by thinking a good thought. We never become good by not doing things, but by filling life with lovely things." [38]

Don't try in your own strength to overcome sin in your life. Rest in your relationship with Jesus. Trusting that he will care for you, refining you, until that great day when you will see him face to face, as Paul explained -

> "May God himself, the God of peace, sanctify you through and through. May your whole spirit, soul and body be kept blameless at the coming of our Lord Jesus Christ. The one who calls you is faithful, and he will do it" (1 Th 5:23-24).

If we concentrate our mind on Jesus, the most positive person who ever lived, the negatives of sin will be overcome.

Jesus cares about your needs: Love is giving, not getting. Love is caring, and God cares for you. Since he gave

---

[38] William Barclay' Commentary of N.T. Luke 11 The Peril of the Empty Soul; Page 153

us Jesus, to die that we might be free, surely with him he will give us also everything we need. Paul reassures us of this fact -

> "He who did not spare his own Son, but gave him up for us all – how will he not also, along with him, graciously give us all things?" (Ro 8:32).

Jesus cares about your problems: The Apostle Paul, who knew what it was to suffer agonisingly for his faith, was still able to understand the great love and care Jesus had for him. He encourages us to grasp hold of this truth. We can ask for help when we need it. Not forgetting, while going through our trials, to be thankful for all the wonderful things Jesus has done for us in the past -

> "Do not be anxious about anything, but in every situation, by prayer and petition, with thanksgiving, present your requests to God. And the peace of God, which transcends all understanding, will guard your hearts and minds in Christ Jesus" (Ph 4:6-7).

God can solve your problems if you ask him to, and he can give you peace of mind while he works things out for you.

Here is my experience of God's tender care when I was in great distress.

When my husband was first invited to Sydney to join Alan Langstaff and his *Temple Trust Bible College*, God made it clear to us that we were to go, and so we did. However, what I did not realise was that after sixteen years in Tasmania, and the strong friendships we had made there, I would go through a grieving period which was very painful. I had lost my position as pastor's wife, I had sadly to leave my friends, and also to leave my home. I became so depressed that I was convinced that God wanted me to die. I felt useless and a burden to my family. Even though I was busy working and caring for my family, and was certainly not useless, that was how I felt. Later I heard that missionaries often go through a similar period of grieving when they go to their first field of service. God evidently uses these times of loss to prepare us to grow closer to him and realise our complete dependence on him.

Thankfully, God spoke to me one day as I was walking in our garden. I heard him very clearly, "Don't you realise if I wanted you to die all I would have to do is take away your breath? I do not want you to die!" Straight away I felt such relief! I knew that he was telling me the truth and my burden of sorrow and depression lifted and I was set free.

After two years in Sydney Alan Langstaff and his family decided to move to the USA, and they wanted us to go with them for an uncertain period of years. After I prayed earnestly over many days God spoke to me again and gave me a promise that if, after two years in USA, I wanted to come home, then he would make it possible. So, I was able to make this second move, even further from my family and friends.

Once more I suffered the same sorrow and depression at parting from everything familiar, but the Lord helped me. The experience I had this time was different. I felt I was being peeled, like an onion, layer after layer. Everything I thought I knew after thirty years as a Christian was sifted until I felt my inner being naked and exposed. However, when I reached the deepest point, I found that Jesus was there. He built me up again, restored me, and gave me a new start to minister for him.

After the two years we did get an invitation to go back to Australia from Bishop Harry Westcott, then the leader of Vision in Australia, but by that time I realised we needed to stay longer. Eight more years went by before we returned home, and during those years we met Dr. Stan DeKoven, who joined his Bible College with ours to make Vision

International College, which is now called (in the USA) VITEN (*Vision International Training and Education Network*). In Australia, a group of schools operate under the generic name *Vision Colleges*.

Jesus cares about your deliverance from oppression: If we have Jesus, he is the answer to all our problems, no matter how serious or negative. He is all we need for victorious Christian living. Satan will then be overcome as we stand in believing faith -

> "Why, my soul, are you downcast? Why so disturbed within me? Put your hope in God, for I will yet praise him, my Saviour and my God" (Ps 42:5).

The answer that gives the victory is to fix your eyes on Jesus. Look to him, hope in him, and he will transform you slowly but surely. Seek him earnestly, ask Jesus to enter your innermost being, don't hold back from surrendering to him completely.

This is pleasing to God and means deliverance for you without any struggle.

Remember Jesus cares for you in every way, you are important to him. Nothing in your life is too small for him to be interested in. Trust him absolutely and he will prove to be wonderfully true.

Fill your life, your mind, and your subconscious with the living Word of God and gradually you will find his cleansing renewing power working in your life. This will fill you with gratitude for his loving care, and the victory he has won for you.

Now our task is to share what we have learned. All around us there are lonely people, desperate people. People who need to know that God cares for them. God loves us as he loves Jesus –

"Then the world will know that you sent me and have loved them even as you have loved me" (Jn 17:23b).

He loves people and his desire is for them to know he cares for them.

What can we do for our neighbours? We need to realise that individuals must be changed for a community to change. Working from the bottom up, not from the top down. Individuals must come to know the love of God before they can influence their neighbours.

We can pray. Praying saves wasted effort, we must look for quality not quantity in our efforts. We must pray for the leaders of our community no matter who they are, as Paul teaches -

> "I urge then, first of all, that petitions, prayers, intercession and thanksgiving be made for all people – for kings and all those in authority, that we may live peaceful and quiet lives in all godliness and holiness" (1 Ti 2:1-2).

We live in a world of contrasts: On the one hand much wickedness, sins of all descriptions, and on the other hand acts of nobility and service.

We can take a life changing message: A message of God's love and ability to change lives and give people a new start. It has been proved again and again that a dramatic change can come to those who decide to follow Jesus. Tangled lives can be straightened out and made beautiful through the power of the Lord.

We are letters made of flesh and blood that can be read by all: We can show by our caring that God is love. We as Christians have experienced God's love for ourselves. Ordinary people can only see God's love through us, as Paul points out to the Corinthian church -

"You ourselves are our letter, written on our hearts, known and read by everyone" (2 Co 3:2).

Edmund Burke, in a letter to Thomas Mercer made this statement –

"The only thing necessary for the triumph of evil is for good men to do nothing"[39]

How true this is. People have never needed Jesus so much as they do now. Let us do our part, showing Jesus to them by our spirit of love and witness in the community

The understanding and acceptance of the deep love Jesus has for us, the victory this brings, and our obligation to share his love with our neighbours is another sure foundation stone for a balanced Christian life.

---

[39] Edmund Burke (1729-1797), British statesman and political thinker.

Chapter Eight:

The Seeds of Faith

A balanced Christian life includes a robust faith that can move mountains of difficulty. In this chapter we see how to develop that kind of faith in the ability of the Lord.

What is your measure of faith?

> "For by the grace given me I say to every one of you: do not think of yourself more highly than you ought, but rather think of yourself with sober judgment, in accordance with the faith God has distributed to each of you" (Ro 12:3).

Faith is like a seed that can grow and develop just as the seeds we plant grow and develop into mature plants. The miracle of plants growing into fruition is truly remarkable. Each seed is programmed to produce after its kind and the nutrients and water drawn up by the roots of the plant bring it to maturity. The creator has done all things well and there is no skint in his multiplication of fruit from the seed planted.

> "We can count how many seeds in an apple but only God knows how many apples can come from one seed." [40]

I learned how prolific God the great Creator is when I began gardening. Planting bean seeds produced so many beans I had to give the extras away to my neighbours.

---

[40] A quote from Robert Schuller.

In the same way, but in a spiritual sense, the seed of our faith grows and proliferates as we feed and water it with the Word of God, and as we pray and see our prayers answered.

"Whatever the mind of man can conceive, and believe, he can achieve." [41]

That statement is a true one which has been proved many times and it is amazing what wonderful discoveries have been achieved by men and women throughout history.

For the Christian seeking to grow in faith, everything God does starts with a seed planted, and he has shown us the way to achieve the kind of faith that moves mountains of difficulty -

"Ask and it will be given to you; seek and you will find; knock and the door will be opened to you. For everyone who asks receives; the one who seeks finds; and to the one who knocks, the door will be opened" (Mt 7:7-8).

- It is the one who asks that receives.
- It is the one who seeks that finds.
- It is the one who knocks that goes through the door when it is opened for them.

Do you want to do something for God?

If you can see yourself doing something for God and if you have received the abilities and the gifts for what you want to achieve, then you can do it! However, we must all face reality!

We are not all called to build a university like Oral Roberts. Or be a great scientist like Albert Einstein, or a great missionary like David Livingstone. But we can do what God has ordained for us before the foundation of the world -

---

[41] A quote from *Think and Grow Rich* by Napoleon Hill

> "For we are God's handiwork, created in Christ Jesus to do good works, which God prepared in advance for us to do" (Ep 2:10).

We are saved for a reason and it is up to us to find that reason – God's plan for our life – and then to complete our task. Indeed, the life of faith can be a time of exciting discovery.

Here is a poem to inspire your faith. These words were written on a poster my husband received at a USA conference for pastors and leaders. He brought it home and hung it on the wall of his office.

It was an inspiration, among many other words of guidance from the Lord, that gave him the confidence to begin writing his books for our Vision Colleges.

> "When faced with a mountain I will not Quit!
> I will keep on striving
> Until I climb over,
> Find a pass through,
> Tunnel underneath,
> Or simply stay and turn the mountain
> Into a miracle with God's help"![42]

Rewarded faith: -

> "Without faith it is impossible to please God, because anyone who comes to him must believe that he exists and that he rewards those who earnestly seek him" (He 11:6).

In his book on prayer, Philip Yancey tells us that six out of ten Americans believe in miracles. More than half of USA doctors report observing miracles in their patients that defy medical explanation.

---

[42] *Possibility Thinker's Creed* by Robert H. Schuller.

An official double-blind experiment has proved prayer works!

Duke and Harvard Universities now have studies on the role of spirituality in health. They have discovered that church goers have a 25% reduction in mortality. Christians live longer because faith works! God rewards those who seek him with their whole heart and refuse to be denied. [43]

> "Dr. Harold G. Koenig, professor of medicine at Duke University reviewed 600 research studies and concluded that people who hold more spiritual beliefs fare significantly better in mental health and adapt more quickly to health problems than those who are less spiritual."[44]

There is no limit to believing faith! Never give up believing that God speaks the truth. When Balaam wanted to curse Israel for Balak, son of Zippor, the king of Moab, for a fee God put these words into his mouth -

> "God is not human, that he should lie, not a human being, that he should change his mind. Does he speak and then not act? Does he promise and not fulfill? I have received a command to bless; he has blessed, and I cannot change it" (Nu 23:19).

Our God is a God who cannot lie, in him there is no shadow of turning. We can trust him completely.

But sometimes we can miss God's best blessing when we give up too soon. We must believe it is God's will to heal no matter what the circumstances. Otherwise we set up a barrier against believing for healing. However, we must acknowledge that God does not always heal, no matter how

---

[43] *Prayer: Does it Make Any Difference?* by Philip Yancey.
[44] *The Biology of Belief* by Bruce H. Lipton, Ph.D. Page 221.

hard we pray. I have attempted to address this mystery in my book *Divine Healing – The Wonder and the Mystery*.[45]

Potential faith: There is no limit to the potential of believing faith -

> "Now faith is confidence in what we hope for and assurance about what we do not see. This is what the ancients were commended for. By faith we understand that the universe was formed at God's command, so that what is seen was not made out of what was visible" (He 11:1-3).

Here we are told that God produced everything from nothing by his command!

The atomic structure, electrons and neutrons, with their central nucleus, are the building blocks of the world we see around us. Theoretically there are vast spaces in objects that look and feel so solid to us. The microcosm and the macrocosm are built the same way. The tiniest atom and the great universe around us have the same fundamental structure.

Scientists tell us that, if we could get far enough away from the universe, to make an observation, it would look exactly like an atom, with the exact same pattern of protons and neutrons spinning around a nucleus. The galaxies seem to be never ending. God is so vast and glorious we should not doubt his ability.

And God created this whole universe by speaking! It is equally certain that God can speak his Word to make sickness, disease, pain and despair disappear in a moment.

We should have his Word in our hearts and minds so we can speak it in faith if there is a need.

---

[45] Vision Publishing 2006

Jesus said to his disciples –

"I have given you authority to trample on snakes and scorpions and to overcome all the power of the enemy; nothing will harm you" (Lu 10:19).

To trample gives the idea of daily rebuke and the Healing Rooms I observed in San Diego used this principle. Sometimes workers trained in prayer for the sick would pray for a person for up to thirty times before healing came. People were encouraged to keep on coming for prayer until the victory was won.

During our time as pastors we saw many wonderful healings, but not everyone was healed and sometimes people died. We concluded that God is sovereign and that no one is meant to live forever in this world of ours.

When our son-in-law David died suddenly the Lord led me to this verse in Job -

"A person's days are determined; you have decreed the number of his months and have set limits he cannot exceed" (Jb 14:5).

And we know also that -

"Precious in the sight of the LORD is the death of his faithful servants" (Ps 116:15).

But you get what you preach for. If you want to see healing, then you must preach healing as God told the youthful Jeremiah -

"I am watching to see that my word is fulfilled" (Je 1:12b).

In my experience God seems to grant more healing in third world countries where people lack the health facilities we enjoy here in Australia. Especially where the healing gospel is taught in places where it has never been preached before. Scott McKinney, a healing evangelist, has observed that once one healing occurs during an evangelistic campaign in a new area, then faith rises in the people and many more healings occur.

Persuaded faith: Abraham knew how to believe God -

> "He did not waver through unbelief regarding the promise of God but was strengthened in his faith and gave glory to God, being fully persuaded that God had power to do what he had promised" (Ro 4:20-21).

Abraham was convinced God could give him a son, through his wife Sarah, even though they had both passed the age of being able to produce a child, and God rewarded Abraham for his faith. We too must be persuaded with all our heart that nothing is too hard for God.

After the many wonderful answers to prayer we received during our time in Tasmania we became very strong in faith and this was a good foundation for another wonderful healing my husband, Ken, was able to grasp while we were in the United States. One year, after a period of intense stress, he developed a bleeding ulcer and became very sick. However, he cried out to God during a long night of agony and distress. I have a vivid memory of him walking around and around our bedroom praying in tongues and crying out to God, "Heal me or take me!" God miraculously answered his prayer by granting him life instead of death. Indeed, he made a full and rapid recovery over a few days. The pain went immediately, but he remained very pale for a time as it took a while for his body to replace the blood he had lost during his bout of sickness. He checked with his medical doctor and was told to be careful to watch for any more bleeding over the next few weeks, but our Lord, who does all things well, had granted Ken a complete healing, so he remained well and has had no sign of a stomach ulcer since that time.

Persevering faith: To persevere – to persist in an undertaking despite counter influence, opposition or discouragement -

> "Consider it pure joy, my brothers and sisters, whenever you face trials of many kinds, because you know that the testing of your faith produces perseverance. Let perseverance finish its work so that you may be mature and complete, not lacking anything" (Ja 1:2-4).

When our faith is tested, we either develop perseverance, even in the face of seeming defeat or we give up! God is never defeated, though at times it may seem so to us.

Pastor David Wright who has a church in Cairns, Queensland, Australia testifies that during a recent missionary journey to New Guinea all the patients in a hospital suffering from malaria and cholera were healed through prayer, except one who refused to be prayed for. They were dying but God raised them up!

Proved faith: Proving our faith means to test the quality of it, to ascertain by experiment how real it is.

Jesus was tested by Satan in the desert and he answered each test with the Word of God. He said again and again, 'It is written' (See Lu 4:1-12).

Because he knew his Father, and was filled with his Word, Jesus was able to answer each temptation with confident faith, knowing that victory would ultimately be his.

Our faith grows in strength as we exercise it. Each answer to prayer strengthens our faith for yet more answers to prayer. To reach this level of faith we must follow the example of Jesus. We must quote the appropriate scriptures aloud and memorise them to get them into our spirit, our innermost part.

Faith will always be tested: This testing produces perseverance, and proves our faith, which brings us to maturity in God.

We must live by the Word of God and claim the victory over sickness and defeat by believing what God says in his Word. Even though we may not see immediate results.

Kathryn Khulman had a great healing ministry over many years. When she was asked, "What is faith?" She answered -

> "Faith is not believing what you see but seeing what you believe." [46]

In other words, the healing must be so real to you that you see it as accomplished before it occurs.

Active faith: The definition of having active faith for healing is clear. This active faith is demonstrated when the person who needs healing acts as if the healing is real until it becomes complete.

Active faith can also be experienced in the realm of trusting God for provision.

Gladys Aylward (1902-1970) was a London parlourmaid, who was rejected by the *Inland China Missions Board* to become a missionary to China. They considered she lacked education and was too old to begin learning Chinese. However, determined to obey what she felt to be God's call on her life, Gladys worked hard at two jobs until she had the train fare to pay her own way from Holland through Germany, Poland and Russia, then to Japan by boat and finally to China. When she left England, she had only her luggage, some food, and only two English pounds in a traveller's cheque, which in those days represented a man's wage for one week. Gladys had no financial backing from any

---
[46] A quote heard on U Tube

other source, she only had her faith and her determination to follow the plan she felt the Lord had given to her to become a missionary to China.

She acted out her faith: She did this by starting the journey, trusting God to be with her to bring her safely to her destination. When she finally found Mrs Lawson, the missionary she had come to assist, she had only 30p left of her money. Many times, on her incredible journey Gladys must have wondered if she was in God's will. It was only on looking back at the end of her journey that she could see God had been leading her all the way.

Between them she and Mrs Lawson opened an inn for muleteers as a centre to tell Bible stories. In the years they worked together Gladys was able to learn the Chinese language and begin to tell Bible stories herself.

After Mrs Lawson's death Gladys was left with no income but God honoured her faith once again by making provision for her to continue her missionary work. The Mandarin of Yangchen made her his foot inspector as the government had decreed there was to be no more foot binding for females. This gave her an income and wonderful opportunities to tell the stories of Jesus to Chinese families. [47]

Challenged faith: Victory goes to the bold. Sometimes it is only in looking back as Gladys did, we can see the guiding hand of God, training us to be strong, firm and steadfast, even while going through apparent, and sometimes very real, failures. He does all things well.

> "You need to persevere so that when you have done the will of God, you will receive what he has promised" (He 10:36).

---

[47] *Heroes of the Cross* by Catherine Swift

We learn through the hard times to trust God completely and absolutely and to rely totally on him. We must learn the potential of faith, and then persevere until we gain the victory we need within the will of God.

Jesus always looked for faith: Luke tells the story of the Roman centurion who asked Jesus to heal his sick servant just by speaking a word of healing. He understood that Jesus could heal from a distance because of his authority over all sickness and disease, just as he as a Roman centurion, could command his troops from a distance. Jesus was pleased by his faith -

> "When Jesus heard this, he was amazed at him, and turning to the crowd following him, he said, "I tell you, I have not found such great faith even in Israel" Then the men who had been sent returned to the house and found the servant well" (Lu 7:9-10).

The challenge for us is to believe without wavering. The promise is there; we need to grasp it, believe it, and go on to see great victories in the lives of suffering people.

The ability to believe God's promises and to exercise our faith in his incredible power to heal, deliver, guide and direct is yet another foundation stone in our search for a balanced Christian life.

Chapter Nine:

In the Garden of God

For a balanced Christian life, we must make sure the vessel of our soul is kept whole, with no cracks caused by sin. Giving in to temptations will allow the water of life we hold to dissipate and be lost slowly but surely.

Springs of water: -

"Caleb said, 'I will give my daughter Aksah in marriage to the man who attacks and captures Kiriath Sepher.' Othniel, son of Kenaz, Caleb's younger brother, took it; so Caleb gave his daughter Aksah to him in marriage... (Aksah) replied, 'Do me a special favour. Since you have given me land in the Negev, give me also springs of water'. So Caleb gave her the upper and lower springs (Jg 1:12-13 & 15).

This story is reminiscent of some of the folk stories of a king offering his daughter to a valiant man who will overcome his enemy for him. It is probable that as Othniel and Aksah were cousins they had played together as children. If, as they grew older, they had learned to love one another there is little wonder then that Othniel was keen to win his former playmate as his bride.

Why did Aksah ask her father for springs of water? I believe she wanted to bless and enrich her husband for these springs represented life, health, blessing and prosperity. Caleb gave her what she asked for and more. He gave her the upper and lower springs. He knew that lower springs may fail in the dry season, but upper springs seldom ever fail.

Water is important: It is essential to life. Have you ever imagined being without easy access to water? Before the modern era people had to either buy water from a water carrier, bring it up from a well, or fetch it for themselves from a creek or river.

Our earliest settlers camped by a stream, or else dug a well for water. Today, in this twenty first century, we who live in the First World are truly blessed. It has been calculated that each modern family, no matter how poor, has the equivalent of 100 slaves to provide them with enough water and energy to meet all their needs. In our modern society, we do not need slaves. Because of modern science we have water on tap in our homes and can buy enough electrical energy to run a refrigerator, washing machine and vacuum cleaner beside any other power tools we may need.

We cannot live without water: Neither can we live spiritually without God's eternal springs of living water. If we remain close to God, our source, we will not dry up, but will always overflow with revelation and blessing to pass on to others.

Effective Christian witness springs from Holy Spirit filled wells. Indeed, water represents eternal life in the language of God. Twice in Jeremiah the prophet calls God a 'spring of living water' -

> "LORD you are the hope of Israel; all who forsake you will be put to shame. Those who turn away from you will be written in the dust because they have forsaken the LORD, the spring of living water" (Je 17:13).

"Written in the dust", means those people who forsake the Lord will be forgotten. As the sands move and change with the wind so their footprints will disappear, and no one will ever remember them.

> "My people have committed two sins: they have forsaken me, the spring of living water, and have dug their own cisterns, broken cisterns that cannot hold water" (Je 2:13).

Cisterns, or water tanks: These do not hold flowing spring water but still water. If the water of a container leaks out there is no way to fill it again unless it rains. It has no spring of water to flow into it!

In the same way we should be careful not to allow leaks in our spiritual tank through cracks caused by such things as –

Unbelief: Are we seeking power with God and man? Then let us pray to be delivered from unbelief. Believe God's Word; it will work; God's Word is powerful -

> "Is not my word like fire", declares the Lord, "and like a hammer that breaks a rock in pieces" (Je 23:29).

Neglect and indifference: These are the first cousins of unbelief and we should beware of these two. The wilderness Manna, representing the spiritual food we gain from God's Word, only lasted for one day so we need to read and examine the Word every day (see Ex 16:11-30).

Disobedience: Turning aside from God's way to our own. Many people of God have begun well but faltered here; let us be careful to obey (see 1 Sa 15:22).

These three sins: unbelief; neglect; and disobedience shatter our containers.

However, the first cracks are caused by **pride, selfishness, unforgiveness, bitterness, and anger.**

Broken water tanks: These are containers with cracks in them. If we allow holes or cracks in our spiritual vessel then the power of the Holy Spirit will be lost.

Have you allowed sin to mar your vessel? If so, you will dry up spiritually and be no use to the kingdom of God.

All of us need spiritual power, so let us study to show ourselves approved and present our bodies a living sacrifice to be used by our Lord and Saviour (see 2 Ti 2:15 & Ro 12:1).

What did Paul do to receive power with God? Here are some suggestions discovered in Philippians chapter three.

- He rejoiced whatever happened,
- He watched and prayed,
- He realised his own helplessness,
- He put his hope and trust in Christ alone,
- He wanted Christ above all,
- He gave up all else,
- He lived in newness of life,
- He looked forward,
- He kept working,
- He realised he wasn't all he should be,
- He forgot the past,
- He fully obeyed the truth he had.

Here are many ideas we can meditate on. How do we measure up to the life of Paul, that great Apostle of faith?

There is also much we can learn from Isaiah: There are three springs of God for us to contemplate.

A spring of fruitfulness: -

"The poor and needy search for water, but there is none; their tongues are parched with thirst. But I the Lord will answer them; I, the God of Israel, will not forsake them. I will make rivers flow on barren heights, and springs within the valleys. I will turn the desert into pools of water, and the parched ground into springs" (Is 41:17-18).

We were needy without Christ, now in Christ we are fruitful. Our present task is to lead others to the springs within the valley of God because now we are:

- Fruitful in our Christian life – Ministering with love, joy and peace.
- Fruitful in our service for God – Working with patience, kindness and goodness.
- And fruitful in our soul – Building our character with faithfulness, gentleness (meekness) and self-control (see Ga 5:22-23).

We must be filled with enthusiasm, with perfect trust in the Lord, if we want to lead others to freedom. Because how can we free other people if we ourselves are in chains?

A spring of freedom: This is what the Lord says -

> "In the time of my favour I will answer you, and in the day of salvation I will help you; I will keep you and will make you to be a covenant for the people, to restore the land and to reassign its desolate inheritances, to say to the captives, 'Come out,' and to those in darkness, 'Be free'! They will feed beside the roads and find pasture on every barren hill. They will neither hunger nor thirst, nor will the desert heat or the sun beat down on them. He who has compassion on them will guide them and lead them beside springs of water" (Is 49:8-10).

There are so many today who need freedom and the Lord can provide salvation for their whole being. We must pray for those we know personally, earnestly and persistently, that God will give them a thirst for his springs of living water.

God sets us free through the work of Jesus on Calvary, and he leads us to these springs so we can share them with others. We are set free from any bondage in our own life so that we can tell our story to anyone who will listen.

A spring of restoration: -

"The Lord will guide you always; he will satisfy your needs in a sun-scorched land and will strengthen your frame. You will be like a well-watered garden, like a spring whose waters never fail. Your people will rebuild the ancient ruins and will raise up the age-old foundations; you will be called Repairer of Broken Walls, Restorer of Streets with Dwellings" (58:11-12).

What a lovely phrase, *a well-watered garden*. Plants always grow better, stronger and are more fruitful if there is plenty of water.

As we are healed and restored, we can pray for the healing and restoration of those who live with problems and difficulties. God's waters do not fail.

Living water comes from the Lord himself to bring nourishment to the souls, feelings and emotions of people in need. Jesus our Saviour transforms lives.

We are planted: We have been likened to cisterns or water tanks in Jeremiah and we have discovered springs of water in Isaiah.

We are also compared to trees in Isaiah: -

"I will put in the desert the cedar and the acacia, the myrtle and the olive. I will set junipers in the wasteland, the fir and the cypress together, so that people may see and know, may consider and understand, that the hand of the LORD has done this; that the Holy One of Israel has created It" (41:19-20).

Here we are compared to trees which God himself has planted: All trees are made of wood, have bark, leaves and seed pods of some kind. In a sense they are uniform, being made of the same substance, yet how many different varieties of trees there are in our world.

In the same way we are all human, yet what diversity there is in each of us. Each human being is unique and precious, worth more than the whole world. -

> "What good will it be for someone to gain the whole world, yet forfeit their soul?" (Mt 16:26).

Each of the trees mentioned in Isaiah that are growing by the springs of living water in the garden of God have a unique quality which we can see reflected in the church today.

Trees that grow in adverse circumstances, such as on the snow line of a mountain, grow at a slower pace, but they also grow stronger because of the cold weather. In the same way, if we go through trials and difficulties, we will grow stronger because of these adverse circumstances.

Matthew Henry tells us in his Commentary: -

> "He was to be a planter; for the church is God's husbandry. Therefore he will do all this for his people, will cure their wounds, release them out of bondage, and comfort them in their sorrows, that they may be called trees of righteousness, the planting of the Lord, that they may be such and be acknowledged to be such, that they may be ornaments to God's vineyard and may be fruitful in the fruits of righteousness, as the branches of God's planting. All that Christ does for us is to make us God's people, and some way serviceable to him as living trees, planted in the house of the Lord, and flourishing in the courts of our God; and all this that he may be glorified – that we may be brought to glorify him by a sincere devotion and an exemplary conversation (for herein is our Father glorified, that we bring forth much fruit), that others also may take occasion from God's favour shining

on his people, and his grace shining in them, to praise him, and that he may be forever glorified in his saints."[48]

Why does God use trees? Nothing in the Bible is there by chance, God knows everything and chooses to speak through his prophets in various ways. Isaiah was inspired to use different trees to reflect God's people and a psalmist also was inspired to see the righteous as trees bearing fruit -

> "The righteous will flourish like the palm tree, they will grow like a cedar in Lebanon; planted in the house of the LORD, they will flourish in the courts of our God. They will still bear fruit in old age, they will stay fresh and green, proclaiming, "The Lord is upright; he is my Rock, and there is no wickedness in him" (Ps 92:12-15).

Let us see what we can learn from the trees God planted.

The Cedar: Strong, durable, sheltering, fruitful, this tree can reflect those who are strong in the eternal Word of God.

What a marvellous tree the cedar is, so versatile and strong. Its roots go down deep into the soil until they reach the water table. Then they draw water for life, and nothing can shake them.

This is what happens when we get into the Word of God, we encounter the fresh streams of the life of God and then nothing can shake our faith. No matter what happens in life we go on serving God and in turn we help others to learn of the wonders of his Word.

During the Second World War: I read of some wartime prisoners in one of the prison camps who between them represented many different denominations. Not having a Bible, they spent time trying to remember all the verses of

---

[48] Matthew Henry's Commentary; Isaiah 60:21

scripture they could. They managed to compile quite a few. I wondered how many I would be able to remember in those same circumstances?

Imagine if all our Bibles were to disappear, how many verses would we be able to recall? It would be an interesting exercise to sit down some time and test yourself just to see how many you can remember.

The Word of God is powerful: It is everlasting, and it produces fruit. It brings revelation and understanding. It changes us! The more we have stored in our memory to meditate on the more revelation knowledge we will experience.

> "For the Word of God is alive and active. Sharper than any double-edged sword, it penetrates even to dividing soul and spirit, joints and marrow; it judges the thoughts and attitudes of the heart" (He 4:12).

The cedar tree also indicates strength, for it can last up to two thousand years. Cedar wood was originally used for the doors of St. Peter's in Rome, though the doors are now replaced by brass doors. Solomon used it too for the building of the Temple.

The cedar tree is used for food by birds and deer. It is a wind break and a bird habitat. It can be used for medicine, oil, perfume and disinfectant and its root meaning in Arabic is "kedre" meaning "power". So, the cedar can speak to us of ministries of strength and power and healing.

The Acacia: The wattle, is a beautiful tree. It was used for the *Ark of the Covenant.* The wood is hard and heavy and indestructible by insects and Moses was instructed to cover the *Ark of the Covenant* in gold. The lid of the Ark was known as the *Mercy Seat.* This represented the mercy of the Lord and each year the High Priest sprinkled the blood of the sacrifice there to cleanse the nation of Israel. Now, because of the sacrifice of Jesus on the cross and the blood he shed we can receive forgiveness, and rejoice in our salvation from sin, without continuous animal sacrifices.

Because the acacia was used for the *Ark of the Covenant* and the *Mercy Seat* it speaks of God's mercy and forgiveness to those who accept Jesus as Saviour. God's mercy is also found in ministries of mercy. There are Christians who feed the hungry and clothe the naked and they will be rewarded. With its gold covering *The Ark of the Covenant* can speak too of the beauty of the bride of Christ and our destiny as we are indestructible if we belong to his church.

This beautiful tree was also used for the *Altar of Incense,* also covered in gold, which stood just outside the Holy of Holies. At the times of prayer, the priest would burn some incense on this *Altar of Incense,* and this speaks to us of the intercessory prayers of the saints. So, the acacia tree also reflects our need to pray and intercede. Prayers for family and friends, and prayers for the church. At times the Holy Spirit may bring the name of someone you know to your mind and you feel the need to pray for them, then afterwards you discover your prayers were needed -

> "The smoke of the incense, together with the prayers of God's people, went up before God from the angel's hand" (Re 8:4).

We should pray also for those in authority, those in government, for world leaders, for God to give them wisdom to make the right decisions or to remove them and put his choice in their place if necessary. There is also a great need to pray for repentance and revival to come; first, to the church, because judgment begins with the church; and then to the world. We are seeing signs of a great outpouring occurring in the third world, in Iran, South America, Africa and Indonesia. We need to pray for Europe, England, the

USA, Australia and other first world countries who need revival desperately as well.

The incense filled the tabernacle during the morning and evening times of prayer, and we are told that our prayers are as incense before the Lord -

> "The four living creatures and the twenty-four elders fell down before the Lamb. Each one had a harp and they were holding golden bowls full of incense, which are the prayers of God's people" (Re 5:8).

The Myrtle: This tree is steam distilled for its perfume which is more exquisite than the rose. Every part, leaves, flowers and twigs are used to make the perfume.

It indicates love, life and vitality and is used in bridal bouquets. The Jews still use Myrtle to adorn their booths and sheds at the Feast of Tabernacles.

The Myrtle can speak to us of the death of Jesus and his suffering, as well as the beautiful perfume of his life. It can also speak to us of our love for God, of his love for us, and of the love we have for our brothers and sisters in Christ. It also speaks of those who by their life and witness reflect the love of God to those who have not yet accepted Christ.

The Olive: This tree has healing qualities, and was recommended for healing mental illness, ulcers, earaches, and gastritis by Hippocrates, the father of modern medicine. Today research has shown there is a scientific basis for many of these beliefs. Modern scientists have also discovered that olive oil prevents insulin resistance and ensures better control of sugar in the blood. Olive oil is part of the Mediterranean diet which has been proved to be the healthiest diet of all.

Have you ever harvested olives? Before the days of automation, our family had a holiday beach house. There was an olive tree on the property and to harvest the olives we were instructed to lay a large canvas beneath our olive tree and then those of us who were harvesting used sturdy rods to bash the tree repeatedly. This caused the olives to fall to the canvas where they could be gathered into buckets and later preserved.

The bashing of the tree to harvest the olives can speak to us of the sufferings of our Lord and the healing quality of the oil speaks of his healing power which he has delegated to us -

> "Is anyone among you sick? Let them call the elders of the church to pray over them and anoint them with oil in the name of the Lord" (Ja 5:14).

Here we are told we should anoint the sick with oil. The olive tree surely reflects those with a healing ministry who seek out and offer to pray for the sick, and it can speak to us of the healing gift in the church so much needed today. We must raise our faith to see God work in mighty miracles, providing a witness to people that our God is the only true God.

The Fir or Pine tree: This is an easily worked tree used for ships masts and general carpentry. The seeds of the Stone Pine are used as food, its large edible seeds resemble the hazelnut. In the Apostle Paul's time, they were preserved in honey.

The Fir can speak to us of the ministry of 'helps' in the church, those who work hard for the Lord in practical ways. Servers are those very essential people who are humble and willing to assist in any way they are needed.

Nothing is too hard for them, they are eager to offer their expertise, whatever that may be, so that the church can run smoothly. We thank God for them, they are pillars of the church and give generously of their time and money. They use their gifting for the edification and strengthening of the church -

"We have different gifts, according to the grace given to each of us. If your gift is prophesying, then prophesy according to your faith; if it is serving, then serve; if it is teaching then teach, if it is to encourage, then give encouragement; if it is giving, then give generously; if it is to lead, do it diligently; if it is to show mercy, do it cheerfully" (Ro 12:6-8).

The Cypress: This tree is like the pine but has a harder and more durable wood which, in Bible days, was used to make musical instruments for temple worship. The Cypress can speak to us of worship. The sound of beautiful musical instruments bringing praise to the Lord, coupled with the sound of human voices lifted in praise and adoration to the God of the Universe, the Maker of all things -

"Praise the LORD. Praise God in his sanctuary; praise him in his mighty heavens. Praise him for his acts of power; praise him for his surpassing greatness. Praise him with the sounding of the trumpet, praise him with the harp and lyre, praise him with timbrel and dancing, praise him with the strings and pipe, praise him with the clash of cymbals, praise him with resounding cymbals. Let everything that has breath praise the LORD. Praise the LORD" (Ps 150).

We should also appreciate the worship leaders who work hard to prepare for each meeting. and pray for them to receive inspiration, through the Holy Spirit, to write songs that will bless the church. I know three people personally who have received a song through the inspiration of the Holy Spirit and there are many these days who are so blessed by the Lord.

A beautiful chorus came to my husband Ken on his way home from lecturing on *The Doctrine of God*, in Crusade Bible College around 1960. He came home and picked out the tune on his banjo mandolin. His chorus has spread around the world and blessed many people –

> "Fill my eyes O my God with the vision of the cross,
> Fill my heart with love for Jesus the Nazarene,
> Fill my mouth with thy praise,
> Let me sing through endless days,
> Take my will, let my life be wholly thine."[49]

The Church: What a wealth of symbolism for the church is in the trees of Isaiah.

- Strength and power through the Word.
- The mercy of God and mercy ministries.
- The perfume of prayer and intercession.
- The love of Jesus and our love for one another.
- Healing and miracles.
- The ministry of helps.
- Worship and adoration.

God chose these trees we have looked at to represent his people and his provision for them. God loves our service, he loves to hear us worship with music and song, and to see us using our spiritual gifts to uplift his people. He rejoices when he sees us give of our time and money to honour him.

The Lord is our *"Spring of Living Water"* and we are likened to *"Trees"* planted in his church body. As we grow into maturity in his well-watered garden, we become ever more fruitful in his service. One day we know we will dwell with him in glory -

> "For the Lamb at the centre of the throne will be their shepherd; he will lead them to springs of living water" (Re 7:17).

---

[49] Chorus by Ken Chant; from The Resource Chorus Book 1990

The Lord, the *"Spring of Living Water"* flowing through our Christian life, helps us to grow in grace and develop our ministry gifts, indicated by the trees of Isaiah, thus keeping the balance we need to continue serving him faithfully.

Chapter Ten:

Jonah's Trials

A balanced Christian life must be a life of daily repentance, being certain that there is no sin in our life, blocking our prayers. In the story of Jonah, we see repentance in action, and the reward of repentance.

God's mercy revealed: This is a dramatic story, which reveals much of the love and mercy of God and is very relevant for Christians today!

But first, as a matter of interest, note how the Jewish Rabbis studied Old Testament books like Jonah.

The teaching of the Rabbis: For the devout and scholarly Jew and especially for the Rabbis, scripture had more than one meaning, and it is true to say that the literal meaning was often regarded as the least important. According to the Rabbis there were four meanings in the Hebrew text. [50]

- Peshat – the simple or literal meaning.
- Remaz – the suggested meaning.
- Derush – the meaning evolved and deduced by investtigation.
- Sod – the **allegorical** meaning.

What is an allegory?

"An **allegory** is the expression, by means of symbolic fictional figures and actions, of truths or generalisations

---

[50] William Barclay's Commentary on N.T. *An Old Story and a New Meaning;* Galatians Page 44.

about human existence. It is a symbolic representation."
[51]

Hidden meanings: The first letter from the four meanings used by the Rabbis, Peshat, Remaz, Derush and Sod (PRDS) are the consonants of the word 'Paradise' (both in Hebrew and English).

The Rabbis believed that when a man succeeded in penetrating into these four different meanings, he had indeed reached the joy of Paradise.

We have noted already that, to the Rabbis, the summit and the peak of all meanings was the fourth, Sod - the allegorical meaning. It would therefore often happen that the Rabbis would take a simple bit of historical narrative from the Old Testament, and would read into the story inner meanings, which often appear to us fantastic, but which were very convincing to the people of their day.

The Apostle Paul used this method: Paul was a trained Rabbi, and he used allegory in Galatians 4: 21-5:1. He explains that the story of Abraham, Sarah, Hagar, Ishmael and Isaac is an allegory of our release from the law. If you read through the verses in Galatians, you will see quite easily how Paul used the story.

Jonah's background: Jonah is mentioned in 2nd Kings -

"(Jereboam)...was the one who restored the boundaries of Israel from Lebo Hamath to the Dead Sea, in accordance with the Word of the LORD, the God of Israel, spoken through his servant Jonah son of Amittai, the prophet from Gath-Hepher" (2 Kg 14:25).

Jonah was a real person, a prophet as well as a statesman. A native of Gath-Hepher he lived in the reign of Jereboam 2nd

---

[51] Webster's Dictionary

(in the 8th century BC) and helped to recover some of Israel's territory, lost before to the Assyrians.

> "If confirmation is required outside the pages of the Bible, it may be worth noting that Gath-Hepher is now identified with a village named El Meshed some miles north of Nazareth, in Zebulon, where according to a firm tradition dating back to Jerome's time, the tomb of Jonah is pointed out even to this day."[52]

He probably did write the book of Jonah: It was usual for the prophets to write in the third person as this book is written. Who else but Jonah would know the excruciating details of his suffering and desperate prayers of repentance while in the belly of the great fish!

> "The view most espoused by conservatives is that the book is history. Except for chapter two the book is concerned exclusively with events that happened in the life of Jonah."[53]

The city of Jonah's call: Nineveh was the capital of the Assyrian Empire – a world empire for 300 years from 900-607 BC., and it is true that Assyria did gradually absorb and destroy the Northern Kingdom of Israel.

The people of the Assyrian nation were very cruel. After sacking a city, they would flay their prisoners alive or pierce them with stakes.

They worshiped the goddess Ishtar!

Doom to Nineveh: Jonah was called to preach doom to the enemy nation, which was already in the process of

---

[52] Explore the Book by J. Sidlow Baxter; Volume 4; Page 148
[53] *The Zondervan Pictorial Encyclopedia of the Bible*; Volume Three; Jonah; Page 677

exterminating his own nation! No wonder he ran away to Tarshish, 2,000 miles from Nineveh.

Now, having laid a good foundation we can look at the book of Jonah, using the method of the Jewish Rabbis.

Peshat; the literal meaning: The simple story is that Jonah was called by God to preach judgment to Nineveh, but he refused and ran away. God made sure that through circumstances (the storm and the large fish), Jonah had a second chance to fulfil his task of preaching to Nineveh.

When the people of Nineveh repented and God had mercy on them Jonah was furious and completely disgusted, but God was compassionate, and showed Jonah his reasons for allowing mercy.

Remaz; the suggested meaning: The motive of the book is its implicit rebuke of narrow nationalism, and its appeal for the love of God toward all men -

> "God ... wants all people to be saved and to come to a knowledge of the truth" (1 Ti 2:4)

As a Jew Jonah thought his race was special; chosen to reveal God to the world, and in a sense that was true; however, no race is special to God. All are loved, and now in this gospel age the church has been given the task of revealing God to the world.

Derush; the meaning deduced and evolved by investigation: There is so much in this story that we can research and discover!

First, the lesson is that we can't run away from God. He is everywhere and in control of everything. He is Sovereign! We read this in the Psalms -

> "Where can I go from your Spirit? Where can I flee from your presence? If I go up to the heavens, you are there; if

I make my bed in the depths, you are there. If I rise on the wings of the dawn, if I settle on the far side of the sea, even there your hand will guide me, your right hand will hold me fast" (Ps 139:7-10).

Second, God can use the elements if he deems it necessary for his will to be done. In the terrible storm the sailors tried hard to save Jonah, but finally they had to sacrifice him to save themselves. (see Jo 1:11-17). God doesn't necessarily create the weather, but he can! For instance, he prophesied drought would be the result for the children of Israel if they were disobedient to his laws (see De 11:17).

Third, God, the creator of all things, prepared a great fish. This indicates something rather special, not necessarily a whale, but a fish large enough to accommodate Jonah and keep him alive for three days.

One account in history: Here is a story indicating the possibility of a man surviving being swallowed by a whale, though only for a short time. This incident was related by Sir Francis Fox and carefully investigated by two scientists. One of the scientists was M. de Parville, the scientific editor of the *Journal des Debats* of Paris.

In February 1891 The Whale ship *Star of the East* was in the vicinity of the Falkland Islands. A seaman, James Bartley, was lost at sea but was recovered the day after from the stomach of a whale caught by the whalers. He was still living but for two weeks after this rescue he was a raving lunatic. Treated kindly by the captain and officers of the ship he gradually regained possession of his senses over a period of three weeks and then resumed his duties.

> "During his time in the whale's stomach Bartley's skin, where exposed to the action of the gastric juice, underwent a striking change. His face, neck, and hands were bleached to a deadly whiteness and took on the appearance of parchment. Bartley affirms that he would

probably have lived inside his house of flesh until he starved, for he lost his senses through fright and not from lack of air." [54]

We can see from this story that Jonah's survival in a whale may have been possible, even for as long as three days. However, try to imagine how depressing three days and three nights in the dark of the fish's belly would have been, though there may have been slight or intermittent light. Only Jonah's strong faith in God could have kept him from despair.

Fourth, God listens to a heart full of faith. He is merciful (see Jo 2:7-9).

Jonah made a faith statement in his adversity -

"I have been banished from your sight; yet I will look again toward your holy temple" (Jo 2:4).

Jonah was determined to worship the Lord, even though he felt himself to be at death's door. How fixed are we to follow the Lord no matter what adversity strikes us? Calamity can make or break a person. Crisis shows our true heart attitude.

Jonah prayed very earnestly -

"When my life was ebbing away, I remembered you, LORD, and my prayer rose to you, to your holy temple" (Jo 2:7.)

Jonah prayed a prayer of faith: Are we able to declare the glory of God even when we have come to the end of ourselves and our own strength? Even when we don't understand why we are suffering? We must continue always to trust God no matter what happens to us.

---

[54] *Explore the Book*; by J. Sidlow Baxter; Volume Four; Page 153

Jonah spoke in faith, as if his prayer for deliverance was answered already: -

> "But I, with shouts of grateful praise, will sacrifice to you. What I have vowed I will make good. I will say, Salvation comes from the LORD". (Jo 2:9).

Jonah gave himself in dedication: He was determined to make good his vow to obey God's command to preach to Nineveh. Can we, in faith, dedicate ourselves to God, and return to following his will for our life if we have taken a wrong direction, as Jonah did?

It was his heart attitude and his decision to return to God's will for his life that brought victory to Jonah. Those who want a similar victory must also be determined to live by faith, to pray the prayer of faith, and to dedicate themselves to God's will for their life -

> "And the Lord commanded the fish, and the fish vomited Jonah onto dry land" (Jo 2:10).

After the three days Jonah is suddenly vomited out on to the shore. It is more than probable that it was Jonah's presence that caused the fish to vomit but the moment and the place were in God's timing. Jonah must have been very pale and smelled strongly of fish. His skin would have been wrinkled and his hair may have gone grey.

We are not told exactly where Jonah was returned to the shore, but after his spectacular arrival he must have become quite famous! It took some time for him to recover from his ordeal, and meanwhile his story would have spread through the testimony of the sailors who had experienced the saga. They would have told of the violent storm, and the calm that followed when they threw Jonah into the raging waters.

Nineveh was 500 miles inland, but there were travelling merchants who may have carried the incredible story of Jonah and the fish back to that city.

We are not told how long between Jonah's return to dry land and his second call to Nineveh, but this time Jonah did not dare to disobey and fulfilled his task (see Jo 3:1-5).

Nineveh repents: The people of Nineveh believed Jonah's message and began to repent. Their repentance was full and complete, with fasting. Even the animals were made to fast! (see Jo 3:6-9).

Perhaps the repentance of the people of Nineveh was assured by the fact that Jonah came to them after being vomited up by the large fish!

It is never too late to repent and seek God's mercy. God listens to the extravagant repentance of the people of Nineveh and decides not to destroy them (see Jo 3:10).

Jonah's reaction was not godly: -

> "Jonah was furious. He lost his temper. He yelled at God, 'God! I knew it – when I was back home, I knew this was going to happen! That's why I ran off to Tarshish! I knew you were sheer grace and mercy, not easily angered, rich in love, and ready at the drop of a hat to turn your plans of punishment into a program of forgiveness!
>
> "So, God, if you won't kill them, kill me! I'm better off dead!"
>
> God said, 'What do you have to be angry about?' (Jo 4:1-4 Message Bible).

It is probable that Jonah's anger came from his conviction that his reputation as a prophet had been damaged beyond repair because his prophecy had not come to pass. (see De 18:21-22).

God shows his compassion by not being angry with Jonah's complaint. He lovingly explains his reasons for showing mercy by the example of the plant (Jo 4: 5-11).

Through Jonah's story we are made aware:
- That God is everywhere.
- That he can control the elements to bring about his will.
- That he listens to a repentant heart full of faith.
- It is never too late to repent and seek God's mercy.
- God is compassionate. He has compassion on Jonah and does not rebuke him for his anger, because God hates hypocrites and prefers us to be real with him, and he appreciated Jonah's honesty.

Sod; The allegorical meaning: Jesus himself uses the story of Jonah in this fashion in Matthew's gospel -

"A wicked and adulterous generation asks for a sign! But none will be given it except the sign of the prophet Jonah. For as Jonah was three days and three nights in the belly of a huge fish, so the Son of Man will be three days and three nights in the heart of the earth. The men of Nineveh will stand up at the judgment with this generation and condemn it; for they repented at the preaching of Jonah, and now something greater than Jonah is here" (Mt 12:39-41).

What can we learn from the story of Jonah?
- That God loves all races of men and desires that all should repent and turn to him. And we see the willingness of the Gentile sailors, and then the people of Nineveh, to listen to a message from God and repent sincerely.

Our Immigrants: In Australia, with so many people seeking asylum from terrorism, we are surrounded by other nationalities. We no longer need to go into all the world to preach the gospel, the world has come to us! Now we need to learn how to approach these immigrants from other nations and tell them the good news of the gospel.

Repentance brings blessing:

The sailors, who tried at first to save Jonah, repented and they were given their life.

Jonah repented and was given a second chance to obey God.

The people of Nineveh repented, and they were given a reprieve from doom at that time, though many years later they reverted to their evil ways and were overcome by the Babylonians.

The Mary Sisters: This Lutheran sisterhood was started after the Second World War. So many soldiers had been killed that few women were able to find a marriage partner. Those Christians who saw no possibility of finding a spouse, established a Convent where they could pray and seek the Lord for others.

The Mary Sisters live by repentance and faith. If their support dries up, they spend time in repentance, seeking the Lord for the reason. When they discover the problem and spend time in repentance, money and supplies recommence.

Smith Wigglesworth, the great Healing Evangelist, took communion every day and read no other book than the Bible. In this way he made sure that he was always in the right place with God, ready to be used in his healing ministry. Though we may not agree with Wigglesworth's reading habits, nonetheless we can live a life of repentance before the Lord, thus enabling him to work through us any time there is a need.

An attitude of daily repentance, bringing with it the forgiveness and blessing of God, is yet another necessary and important foundation stone for balancing our Christian life.

Chapter Eleven:

The Path To Victory

We live a life of balance by learning how to live victoriously and by disciplining our mind and emotions to live by the Word of God.

Quotes from some famous men:

Abraham Lincoln: A United States President: -

"I believe the Bible is the best gift God has ever given to man. All the good from the Saviour of the world is communicated to us through this book."

Sir William Herschel: A German born British astronomer and composer: -

"All human discoveries seem to be made only for the purpose of confirming more and more strongly the truths contained in the Sacred Scriptures."

Horace Greely: Founder and editor of the New York Tribune: -

"It is impossible to enslave mentally or socially a Bible reading people. The principles of the Bible are the ground-work of human freedom."

John Ruskin: Leading British art critic and philanthropist of the Victorian era: -

"Whatever merit there is in anything that I have written is simply due to the fact that when I was a child my mother daily read me a part of the Bible and daily made me learn a part of it by heart."[55]

These men understood the power of the Bible and what it can do for the one who reads and meditates on its message.

We should read it aloud: By reciting parts of this wonderful Word, we can guard our mind and emotions from Satan. Also, learning by heart verses of scripture enables the Holy Spirit to remind us of them, thus helping us to gain victory over Satan's deceitful attacks.

Bringing every thought captive -

"For though we live in the world, we do not wage war as the world does. The weapons we fight with are not the weapons of the world. On the contrary, they have divine power to demolish strongholds. We demolish arguments and every pretension that sets itself up against the knowledge of God, and we take captive every thought to make it obedient to Christ" (2 Co 10:3-5).

The background to these verses is that Paul was under attack from false apostles who envied him and tried to undermine his leadership. Paul knew to look at the spiritual aspect of the attack and to see the motivation behind the words of the dishonest apostles. It was Satan using them to disrupt his ministry.

In the battle for our mind and emotions we must fight using the Word of God. Bringing every negative thought that comes from Satan under obedience to Christ the Living Word. Behind the natural, what is happening around us; we must perceive the true reason for some of our trials; spiritual wickedness in high places. It is Satan who is our enemy.

---

[55] These quotes from Halley's Bible Handbook by Henley H. Halley.

In other words, we must learn to use Scripture to defeat the enemy of our soul, and our four weapons are:

- **The blood of the lamb:** The life Jesus laid down for us on the cross -

"Therefore, brothers and sisters, since we have confidence to enter the Most Holy Place by the blood of Jesus, by a new and living way opened for us through the curtain, that is, his body, and since we have a great priest over the house of God, let us draw near to God with a sincere heart and with the full assurance that faith brings, having our hearts sprinkled to cleanse us from a guilty conscience and having our bodies washed with pure water" (He 10:19-22).

- **The victorious Word of God:** We conquer through the word of our testimony. -

"They triumphed over him by the blood of the Lamb and by the word of their testimony; they did not love their lives so much as to shrink from death" (Re 12:11).

- **The authority of the name of Jesus:** This is given to us who believe -

Jesus said, "I saw Satan fall like lightning from heaven, I have given you authority to trample on snakes and scorpions and to overcome all the power of the enemy; nothing will harm you" (Lu 10:18-19).

- **The power of the Holy Spirit:** -

Jesus said, "You will receive power when the Holy Spirit comes on you; and you will be my witnesses in Jerusalem, and in all Judea and Samaria, and to the ends of the earth" (Ac 1:8).

"The Advocate, the Holy Spirit, whom the Father will send in my name, will teach you all things and will remind you of everything I have said to you" (Jn 14:26).

Jesus came to give us abundant life: He tells us, -

"The thief comes only to steal and kill and destroy; I have come that they may have life and have it to the full" (Jn 10:10).

Satan comes to steal!

- He tries to steal our peace by accusing us of sin
- He tries to steal our joy by causing us to doubt.
- He tries to steal our life by causing depression
- He tries to steal our health by bringing sickness and misery into our life.

Satan comes to destroy!

- He tries to destroy lives
- He tries to destroy marriages and families
- He tries to destroy pastors and churches.

Satan is a liar: Unless we become aware of his plan to defeat us by lies and deception; attacking us through our mind and emotions, we will never gain the victory we desire.

(The devil) "was a murderer from the beginning, not holding to the truth, for there is no truth in him. When he lies, he speaks his native language, for he is a liar and the father of lies" (Jn 8:44b).

Because of this we must learn to live by our will, making right decisions. Our Christian life will always be on a faulty foundation if we live by our emotions instead of the Word of God.

Once we decide to make the Word our foundation; to live by what God says about us, we will be settled in our faith and able to grow in Christ.

Jesus came to destroy the works of the devil! He came to give us back our life and dignity and the ability to control our mind and emotions. He came to give us victory in our Christian life. He came to give us abundance of happiness and joy in our marriage, and in our family and church life.

But we have our part to play. There are battles we may have to fight!

The battle against fear: There are legitimate fears which keep us from danger, and there are fears that may stem from childhood traumas. There is the fear of man which stops some from witnessing to others the good news of the Gospel. Then there are nebulous fears that we do not understand but they attack us just the same.

God promises us power: -

> "For the Spirit God gave us does not make us timid, but gives us power, love and self-discipline" (2 Ti 1:7).

In this verse Paul was inspiring Timothy to grasp the power of God, to encounter dangers and enemies bravely, to bear up under trials, to overcome, to triumph even under persecution, by believing this Word from God.

The word **power** in the Greek is *dunamis* (ability or might), and this is not passive, this is dynamite with the fuse already lit and the explosion begun. This kind of power strengthens us to stand against Satan, and to fortify us against persecution.

Paul advises Timothy again in verse 8,

> "So, do not be ashamed of the testimony about our Lord or of me his prisoner. Rather join with me in suffering for the gospel, by the **power** of God."

It is in the very nature of the Gospel to inspire with holy courage.

John and Elizabeth Stam: These two American missionaries in China, were killed by Communist troops in 1934. Their baby, Helen, was found two days later by a Chinese pastor who took her home and cared for her. The Reverend Lo Ke-chou and his wife then took the baby girl to her maternal grandparents, the Reverend Charles Ernest Scott and his wife, Clara, who were also missionaries in China. The Stams' baby daughter later came to the United States and was raised by her aunt and uncle, George and Helen Mahy. As for Helen's parents, a small group of Christians found their bodies and buried them on a hillside. The Stams' gravestones read:

"John Cornelius Stam, (born) January 18, 1907, That Christ may be glorified, whether by life or by death. Philippians 1:20.

Elisabeth Scott Stam, (born) February 22, 1906. For me to live is Christ and to die is gain. Philippians 1:21."

The story of their martyrdom was much publicized and inspired many to become missionaries. [56]

God has also promised us love: Paul tells Timothy, -

"What you heard from me, keep as the pattern of sound teaching, with faith and love in Christ Jesus" (2 Ti 1:13).

The word **love** in the Greek (*agape*)[57] means good will toward all, which inspires us in our duty to God and our fellow man. Love overcomes fear, we need no longer feel the fear of man or be timid in our witness for Christ. Our faith and love for Jesus become so strong we are bold to speak for him.

---

[56] Wycliffe's Biographical Dictionary of the Church by Elgin S. Moyer
[57] Pronounced "a-GAH-pay".

Last of all God has promised us self-control: -

> "For by the grace given me I say to every one of you: do not think of yourself more highly than you ought, but rather think of yourself with sober (prudent) judgment, in accordance with the faith God has distributed to each of you" (Ro 12:3).

Self-control involves having a disciplined mind. This will enable you to overcome emotions which are destructive, or negative.

However, we need to be cautious:

Love, coming between **power** and **self-control** (sober prudence) stops us from being either too fearful, or to forceful, in our witness for Christ. Too much undisciplined power, without love, and we can blow up, causing spiritual mayhem. Too much self-control (sober prudence) and we can dry up spiritually, becoming useless for God's kingdom.

The balance between these three expressions ensures that we lead a Christian life that is full of courage and good sense.

The battle against depression: So long as depression is not caused by sickness, or by constant pain, then we can overcome it by deciding that we will no longer allow Satan to deceive us or rob us of our abundant life in Christ -

> "Be strong in the Lord and in his mighty power. Put on the full armour of God so that you can take your stand against the devil's schemes. For our struggle is not against flesh and blood, but against the rulers, against the authorities, against the powers of this dark world and against the spiritual forces of evil in the heavenly realms" (Ep 6:10-12).

Remember, your emotions are controlled by your thoughts, and if you replace your thoughts with God's thoughts, then you can be set free from negative emotions.

How do we control our thoughts? By resisting soulish thoughts and filling our mind with the Word of God.

There are also some helps for depression from modern medicine. The doctors' advice? Eat right! Exercise right! Think right! Breathe in lots of oxygen! And scripture warns-

> "Be alert and of sober mind. Your enemy, the devil, prowls around like a roaring lion looking for someone to devour. Resist him, standing firm in the faith" (1 Pe 5:8-9a).

Think right thoughts and your emotions will come into line with your thoughts!

Think about things that are true, noble, right, pure, lovely, admirable, excellent, and praiseworthy (See Ph 4:8).

The brain that changes itself: When we think positively the power of the human brain is amazing, both _for_ positive emotions, and _against_ negative emotions. It has been found recently that the brain can rejuvenate by growing new cells. Amazing things can be achieved by exercising the brain through rote learning. Both positive and negative tracks can be laid down.

People who have had a stroke can exercise to replace the abilities they have lost by activating another part of their brain. [58]

The Creator who made us has made it possible for us to be healed from depression if we will replace our negative emotions with his Word.

---

[58] *The Brain that Changes Itself* by Norman Doig MD

The battle against doubt: -

"Without faith it is impossible to please God, because anyone who comes to him must believe that he exists and that he rewards those who earnestly seek him" (He 11:6).

What can you do when faced with doubts?

- Look at the beauty around you and see God in all creation -

"Since the creation of the world God's invisible qualities – his eternal power and divine nature – have been clearly seen, being understood from what has been made, so that people are without excuse" (Ro 1:20).

- Talk over your doubts with a mature Christian and ask him or her to recommend good books on Christian beliefs. *Strong Reasons* by my husband, Ken Chant, is particularly good concerning proofs of the existence of God. *Who Moved the Stone,* by Frank Morison, is another good book about the truth of Jesus' resurrection from the dead.

- Ask God to lead you to other mature Christians who have answers for your doubts.

- Research the stories of great miracles wrought during the last one hundred years. There are many books now available setting out the history of the many healing evangelists of the 20th Century, such as Evangelist Smith Wigglesworth, already mentioned in a previous chapter.[59]

---

[59] Such as: *Smith Wigglesworth – The Complete Collection of His Life Teachings* by Roberts Liardon; Albury Publishing, Tulsa OK, USA 1996.

The battle against self-pity: The way to overcoming self-pity is by the same path we followed to get rid of negative thoughts and emotions in our life.

We must discipline our mind -

> "Therefore, strengthen your feeble arms and weak knees. Make level paths for your feet, so that the lame may not be disabled, but rather healed" (He 12:12-13).

In the words of the Message Bible -

> "So, don't sit around on your hands! No more dragging your feet! Clear the path for long distance runners so no one will trip or fall, so no one will step in a hole and sprain an ankle. Help each other out and run for it."

Bring your conscious mind into subjection to your spirit by meditating on the Word of God and allow him to fill your mind with his wonder and majesty. Read one of the Psalms, such as *Psalm 34* which is filled with positive energy declaring that God answers prayer and protects his people.

You can control your emotions if you make sure your mind is full of scriptures about victory, which the Holy Spirit can then bring into your consciousness when you need them.

William Tyndale: (1494-1536). The Word of God is precious. Did you know there was a time in the 14th Century when it was death to teach the English Bible?

In England men risked their lives to sit up all night to hear the Bible read to them in their own language!

To provide that first printed Bible in English William Tyndale suffered poverty, exile, bitter absence from friends, hunger and thirst and cold and great dangers. Finally, in

1536 he was arrested and burned to death, for his work in providing the Bible in English to everyone.[60]

There is no other book which has cost so much in suffering. Many were martyred in order to make this precious book available to us.

It is our great privilege to own our Bible and to be able to read it freely.

It is also our great responsibility to learn as much as we can from it to help us to control our mind and emotions.

As we absorb Scripture we are cleansed and healed by God in our deepest memories. He washes our innermost being with his Word:

- In our spirit -

"If anyone is in Christ, the new creation has come. The old has gone, the new is here!" (2 Co 5:17)

- In our mind -

"Do not conform to the pattern of this world but be transformed by the renewing of your mind. Then you will be able to test and approve what God's will is – his good pleasing and perfect will" (Ro 12:2).

- And in our subconscious mind. -

"I pray that out of his glorious riches he may strengthen you with power through his Spirit in your inner being, so that Christ may dwell in your hearts through faith" (Eph 3: 16-17a).

---

[60] *William Tyndale, A Biography* by David Daniell

We have plenty of power to win the battles we face in our Christian life. Jesus the Living Word has won the victory for us. Let us rest in his mighty victory on Calvary.

Then with this knowledge let us go on to claim victory over all the power of the enemy, not only for ourselves but for others.

We can experience this deep-seated victory through reading the Word of God, then meditating on it and endeavouring to memorise it. If we do, then we can build another strong foundation stone for our balanced Christian life.

Chapter Twelve:

Creative Thoughts

Learning to think God's thoughts, and to see this world around us with his eyes, will assist us in learning how to live a life of faith, becoming perfectly balanced and secure in our believing.

Wisdom from man:

Ralph Waldo Emerson: Author:

"A man is what he thinks about all day long."

Marcus Aurelius: (AD 161-180), Roman Emperor:

"A man's life is what his thoughts make it."

Norman Vincent Peale: American minister & author:

"Change your thoughts and you change your world."[61]

Wisdom from God:

For as a man thinks in his heart, so is he (Pr 23:7).

What we think about is important, our life is influenced deeply by our thoughts. The Apostle Paul tells us to think about things that are true, noble, right, pure, lovely, admirable, excellent, and praiseworthy (Ph 4:8). Here is a meditation on this scripture.

> "Our emotions have no will of their own
> they merely follow our will,
> our thoughts and our decisions.

---

[61] Quotes gathered over the years.

> Therefore, we will not think about
> the past which we cannot change,
> nor the future,
> for it has not yet arrived.
> instead we will enjoy the present moment,
> God's beautiful creation,
> and those we love.
> Our emotions will come into line
> with our will, and decisions we make,
> changing to reflect our thoughts.
> They are now positive instead of negative
> happy and cheerful,
> instead of sad and miserable.
> Loving instead of unloving.
> Forgiving instead of un-forgiving.
> We will cease to brood and begin to live,
> victoriously in Christ." *(AMC)*

When we are connected to God, through our acceptance of Jesus' finished work on Calvary, then the Lord has some wonderful things to say about us in Paul's letters. His power can quicken our mortal bodies and energise our spirit, because the same power which raised Christ from the dead dwells in us -

> "If the Spirit of him who raised Jesus from the dead is living in you, he who raised Christ from the dead will also give life to your mortal bodies because of his Spirit who lives in you" (Ro 8:11).

However, like the light bulb, being plugged in is not enough, we must be switched on. We must use the power or lose the power. If we stop using our muscles, we grow weaker and weaker, but if we exercise regularly our muscles grow stronger. In the same way our spiritual life can grow weaker or stronger depending on how we exercise our faith.

How do we switch on this power? Faith and power come through our believing the Word of God -

"Faith comes by hearing the message, and the message is heard through the Word about Christ" (Ro 10:17).

Paul prayed for the Colossian Christians who had heard the Word gladly and had accepted God's grace in all its truth. He told them -

"Since the day we heard about you, we have not stopped praying for you. We continually ask God to fill you with the knowledge of his will through all the wisdom and understanding that the Spirit gives, so that you may live a life worthy of the Lord and please him in every way: bearing fruit in every good work, growing in the knowledge of God, being strengthened with all power according to his glorious might so that you may have great endurance and patience, and giving joyful thanks to the Father, who has qualified you to share in the inheritance of his holy people in the kingdom of light" (Cl 1:9-12).

What encouragement these words give us, to be able to hold this Word of God in our hands and read it anytime is truly a blessing we should cherish.

If we have accepted Christ as Saviour: Then there are solid truths we can hold in our heart, taken from this word written to the Colossians.

1. We can be filled with the knowledge of God's will: -

"He made known his ways to Moses, his deeds to the people of Israel" (Ps 103:7).

God revealed to Moses the reason he did things, the rest of the tribe of Israel were only permitted to observe the results of his decisions. We too can know the mind of God if we search his Word diligently and meditate on it.

2. We can please the Lord in every way. Paul advises the Ephesians: -

"Find out what pleases the Lord" (Ep 5:10).

And he prays for the Colossians to be filled with the knowledge and wisdom of God so that, -

"You may live a life worthy of the Lord and please him in every way" (Cl 1:10).

Moses also pleaded with God: -

"If you are pleased with me, teach me your ways so I may know you and continue to find favour with you" (Ex 33:13a).

We too can seek to please the Lord and ask him to show us his ways. He will hear our prayer and lead us to share his thoughts and see things with his eyes.

3. We can bear fruit in every good work: -

"Never be lacking in zeal, but keep your spiritual fervour, serving the Lord" (Ro 12:11).

Because the fruit of the Holy Spirit is love, joy, peace, patience, kindness, goodness, faithfulness, gentleness, and self-control, then wherever we are, and whatever we are doing, we should be displaying the nature of Christ.

4. We can increase in the knowledge of God: -

"Solid food is for the mature, who by constant use have trained themselves to distinguish good from evil" (He 5:14).

As we read God's Word and meditate on it, we grow in understanding. Constant use of the Word, thinking about it and seeking to understand it fully, is what brings revelation knowledge to expand and strengthen our spirit.

5. We can be strengthened with God's power: -

"Who among the gods is like you, LORD? Who is like you – majestic in holiness, awesome in glory, working wonders?" (Ex 15:11).

It is the Lord who gives us the strength to do his will, we cannot manage without his assistance. Whatever we do must be done in his strength and for his ultimate glory. We can follow the will of God for our life through Christ who strengthens us. (see Ph 4:13).

6. We can show great endurance and patience: -

"Endure hardship as discipline; God is treating you as his children" (He 12:7a).

The Lord has called us to be steadfast in our Christian walk, to continue each day in his strength, accepting his discipline.

7. We can share in the inheritance of the saints in the kingdom: -

"When you believed, you were marked in him with a seal, the promised Holy Spirit" (Ep 1:13b).

The Holy Spirit has been given to us to help us to know God, to have a close relationship with him. When we don't know how to pray, he gives us a prayer language to cry out to the Lord -

"...The Spirit helps us in our weakness. We do not know what we ought to pray for, but the Spirit himself intercedes for us through wordless groans. And he who searches our hearts knows the mind of the Spirit, because the Spirit intercedes for God's people in accordance with the will of God" (Ro 8:26-27).

Learning to live through faith: -

> "So then, just as you received Christ Jesus as Lord, continue to live your lives in him, rooted and built up in him, strengthened in the faith as you were taught, and overflowing with thankfulness" (Cl 2:6-7).

How did we receive Christ? **By faith!** Then that is how we continue. **By faith!**

Strengthened in **the faith,** that is in Christian doctrine, and learning to **live by faith** in God's Word; we learn to mix the Word with faith. If we can learn to live by faith, then we will live in constant victory.

Paul advised the Roman Christians -

> "The Word is near you: it is in your mouth and in your heart, that is, the message concerning faith that we proclaim. If you declare with your mouth, "Jesus is Lord," and believe in your heart that God raised him from the dead, you will be saved. For it is with your heart that you believe and are justified, and it is with your mouth that you profess your faith and are saved" (Ro 10: 8b-10).

This is how we begin our life of faith: We believe with our heart and speak out scripture with our mouth for ongoing victory, just as we believed and confessed for our salvation.

If we continue to believe what God says in his Word with our heart and speak it aloud with our mouth it will become part of us, and victories will come easily. So read the Word, memorise it, meditate on it, confess it, speak it aloud! If you do then Satan will be defeated in your thought life.

One thing we need to note!

We can experience failure if we confuse our faith with our feelings. God works by faith, not by feelings. We must read the facts within God's Word, believe them, then our feelings and emotions will come into line with our believing.

Why? Because our emotions follow our will and our decisions.

How can we apply this way of thinking?

- If you are doubting your salvation be reassured -

"God so loved the world that he gave his one and only Son, that whoever believes in him shall not perish but have eternal life" (Jn 3:16).

- If you doubt God's love for you be comforted -

"Praise be to the God and Father of our Lord Jesus Christ, who has blessed us in the heavenly realms with every spiritual blessing in Christ" (Ep 1:3).

See what great love the Father has lavished on us, that we should be called children of God! And that is what we are! (Jn 3:1a).

- If you doubt your sins are forgiven believe this Word -

"If we confess our sins, he is faithful and just and will forgive us our sins and purify us from all unrighteousness" (1 Jn 1:9).

Search diligently and discover any promise you need in your Bible – and then claim it boldly.

Battle strategies: We must face our enemy to win battles in the life of faith -

"All the nations surrounded me, but in the name of the LORD I cut them down. They surrounded me on every side, but in the name of the LORD I cut them down. They swarmed around me like bees, but they were consumed as quickly as burning thorns; In the name of the LORD I cut them down" (Ps 118:10-12).

Through this very real battle David writes about we can see our own present spiritual battles. Like David, we must face our Satanic adversary and cut him down in Jesus name.

Victory comes when we believe what God says. Satan, our enemy, is overcome when we memorise, and repeat aloud, appropriate verses from the Word of God.

We are God's children, bought with a price, the precious blood of Jesus, and what God says about us in his Word is the truth. He will not change his mind, for he does not change like shifting shadows (see Ja 1:17).

However, testing times come to us all. Testing times came to Jesus, and a servant is not above his master. We too must be tested to prove our determination to persevere with our faith. This testing strengthens us and transforms us into warriors for the Lord.

A challenge: Do you need to believe God for something important to you personally?

If so, here is a challenge to believe, to claim the promise you need, and to ask God for a 'rhema' word.

What is a 'rhema'? It is an up to date word given by God to raise the faith and expectation of the person who needs a miracle, as opposed to the general Word of God. [62]

---

[62] W. E. Vine, *Expository Dictionary of NT Words*; Lowe and Brydon printers; London 1940; Page 230. "The significance of *rhema* (as distinct from *logos*) is exemplified in the injunction to "take the sword of the Spirit, which is the word of God,"Ep.6:17; here the reference is not to the whole Bible as such, but to the individual scripture which the Spirit brings to our remembrance for use in time of need, a prerequisite being the regular storing of the mind with Scripture."

As you pray, ask God to help you to know his mind, to think his thoughts, see with his eyes. Then understanding these aspects, claim the promise you need and go on to victory.

Learning some of the marvellous ways to make use of the Word of God to strengthen your believing faith, forms another foundation stone for a balanced Christian life.

Chapter Thirteen:

Winning by Losing

In this chapter we learn how to win Christian victory by losing ambition and self-will. This leads us on to a greater understanding of the balanced Christian life.

Death experiences: In the natural realm death must come before life can grow and develop. Because of this principle there must be death experiences in the creation of spiritual life as well.

These death experiences come through trials, and crises the Lord allows in our life at various times, to test us and to prove us. He doesn't send them, but he does use them. These trials can be caused by persecution, but usually they are just part of our life in this world.

Please note: These tests are not the same as the trials we bring on ourselves through sin. To suffer as a Christian is one thing, but to suffer if we have done wrong, that is different -

> "If you suffer, it should not be as a murderer or thief or any other kind of criminal, or even as a meddler. However, if you suffer as a Christian, do not be ashamed, but praise God that you bear that name" (1 Pe 4:15-16).

We can see from the Old Testament that the Lord used testing times to train the ancient Israelites. As Moses reminded them -

> "Remember how the Lord your God led you all the way in the wilderness these forty years, to humble and test you in order to know what was in your heart, whether or not you would keep his commands" (De 8:2).

As with the Israelites long ago God allows trials and crises to come into our life both to test us and to help form our Christian character. These experiences reveal who we are and what we have in him. The Lord wants to know if we will follow him no matter what trials we must go through.

There is complete surrender in true spiritual maturity: That is when we become completely dependent on God and his grace. When this happens whatever we accomplish will be by God's grace and ensures he will get all the glory.

Elijah was one of many in Old Testament times who suffered trials. His testing times led to power with God and man. We read of his victory over the priests of Baal in 1 Kings chapter 18.

Elijah was determined to prove to the people who had fallen away from the one true God and begun to worship Baal, that only the God of Israel was God, and that Baal was merely an idol of stone with no power. He proved this admirably by arranging a test with two altars. He challenged the priests of Baal to ask their god to send fire to burn up their offering. They tried all day, calling frantically on Baal to answer them but without result. Then Elijah stepped forward to prove his point by first, pouring water over his offering to make it harder to burn, then calling on the God of Israel to send the fire. The fire of God fell and consumed the animal sacrifice and licked up the water as well until there was nothing left.

Elijah's many years of faithful service culminated in this scene on Mt Carmel. There, in confronting the priests of Baal he proved conclusively that God was Almighty and All powerful, the only true God, but after this wonderful experience Elijah suffered a nervous collapse. He could have led a great revival in Israel if he had remained steady, instead he ran from Jezebel's threat (see 1 Kings 19:2-3).

We cannot blame Elijah for this, although he had been able to give high glory to God through his triumphant victory over the priests of Baal he was, despite his great spiritual strength, only a frail human being. His subsequent collapse would have been caused first, by the deep and profound spiritual experience of calling down the fire of God and second, by the nervous energy of his righteous anger which led to his slaughtering the priests of Baal. After this immense physical and spiritual crisis, he would have been exhausted both in body and in spirit.

Elijah suffered through the usual four stages of crisis after his nervous energy drained away and left him exposed to fear.

- **Impact phase:** – Elijah chooses flight, depression sets in and he wants to die (see 19:3).

- **Withdrawal/confusion:** – He sits under a broom tree depressed and suicidal (see 19:4).

- **Adjustment:** – God understands our frame. He restores Elijah physically, so he will be able and ready to hear when he speaks to him. He does that by sending an angel to give him water and bread. When Elijah wakes from a refreshing sleep the angel feeds him again! The strength he gains is enough for his journey to a safe place (see 19:5-9).

- **Reconstruction/reconciliation:** – In that safe place he learns that God isn't finished with him yet. Through his still small voice the Lord reassures Elijah that he is not alone, there are still 7,000 people in Israel who have not bowed the knee to Baal. He also gives him new tasks to accomplish and a new disciple, Elisha, to train for the future (see 19:10-21).[63]

Through this story we see the compassionate Father heart of God. If we will trust him through each trial, he will deal with us as he dealt with Elijah.

Elijah was given bread, symbolic of the Word of God, and living water, symbolic of the Holy Spirit. These two, the Word and the Spirit, also restore us. After a period of trial or testing, especially if we fail in some way as Elijah did, God may take us through the same three stages he granted Elijah.

- **Spiritual restoration:** – Through our prayers and meditations, he restores us by giving us revelation in his Word and an anointing from his Holy Spirit.

- **Instruction from his Word:** – Through the still small voice that comes as we meditate on his Word, asking for guidance and direction.

- **A new task to perform:** – If we seek the Lord earnestly, he will reveal this to us in his time.

During these times of testing we learn to live by the Word of God and by the guidance of the Holy Spirit, not by our feelings and emotions.

Christians who live on their emotions will always be up and down, and in and out of their Christian experience. We must live instead by what God says about us in his Word. It is not what we feel, but what God says, that is the truth.

God works on the principle of maturity and not by the spirit of want or desire. He is more interested in who we are than

---

[63] From *Crisis Counseling: Hope and Healing for Life's Transitions* by Dr Stan DeKoven ; Vision Publishing 1995.

in what we do for him. Because of this he may sometimes delay the answer to a prayer. He wants to test our faith.

The truth is we grow more depth of character in the valleys of trial than in the mountain tops of blessing.

Too many Christians try Christianity for a few years, then when a trial comes, they give up. The prosperity gospel is at fault here. People who are taught that nothing will go wrong, and they will never get sick, unless they have sin in their life, will try to hide the trial they are going through in case someone accuses them of sin. This will become overwhelming for them; wondering what they have done to deserve their circumstances. They will search for a reason and, if they can't find one, will despair and begin to blame God for their misery. It is little wonder if, after a few years, they abandon the Christian life.[64]

People who are taught properly that trials and tests are permitted by God for training in righteousness and to produce good character will be much more stable in their Christian life.

Search the scriptures: Learn not to be ruled by your feelings but by God's promises. Ask yourself, "What does the Word say?"

So far, we have seen the need to live by the Word of God and by the Spirit of God but if we would be fully mature there is one more thing we need.

Obedience!

> "During the days of Jesus' life on earth, he offered up prayers and petitions with fervent cries and tears to the

---

[64] *God Greed and the Prosperity Gospel* by Costi W. Hinn. I do not mean that there are no promises of prosperity in the Bible, because indeed there are many of them; but, they must be tempered by the equally many promises of trials.

one who could save him from death, and he was heard because of his reverent submission. Son though he was, he learned obedience from what he suffered and, once made perfect, he became the source of eternal salvation for all who obey him" (He 5:7-9).

If we want our prayers to be heard, then we must submit reverently to the dealings of God. We go through life experiences, which sometimes include suffering, pain and sorrow, and they compel us, and teach us, to surrender ourselves unreservedly to God as Jesus did.

Faith versus fatalism: We should not surrender to fatalism, but instead surrender in faith, trusting in the ultimate goodness of God in directing our life because we know that in all things God works for the good of those who love him (see Ro 8:28).

Knowing these things, we can now view a crisis of suffering as a friend that will create deeper priorities in our life. When tragedy does strike, how unimportant things become that before we thought essential!

Broken bread: In our crisis we are broken enough to become completely dependent on God. All our human pride and self-sufficiency are swallowed up. There is no more room for pride.

In the breaking of the old nature new life begins to flow. Jesus is revealed in all his love and compassion. The Holy Spirit gives us revelation by breaking to us the Bread of Life, our Lord Jesus, so we can grow spiritually.

A trial or a crisis does not tell us what we have but what we do not have. It reveals our weaknesses and how much we need God and how much we must hold onto his victory, won for us through Christ.

Leo Harris used to say,

"We only really have what we hold under pressure." [65]

It is important to persevere, to keep on keeping on no matter what happens -

> "We boast in the hope of the glory of God. Not only so, but we also glory in our sufferings, because we know that suffering produces perseverance; perseverance, character; and character, hope" (Ro 5:2b-4).

Suffering, with the right attitude, through trials and crises, builds character into our life and gives us hope for the future. We become strong Christians.

We gain a hunger for God: Suffering also produces a great desire for God and his Word as Moses explained -

> "He humbled you, causing you to hunger and then feeding you with manna, which neither you nor your ancestors had known, to teach you that man does not live on bread alone but on every word that comes from the mouth of the LORD" (De 8:3).

When we are suffering trials, we reach out to the Lord for comfort from his Word, we search diligently for an explanation of what we are going through. The Word becomes our necessary food until we are satisfied that we have found the answer we seek.

We must have a right attitude: If, instead of searching for a Word from scripture during our trial, we rebel against God's dealings, we can become hard and bitter and lose faith.

By contrast, if we have the right attitude and seek God earnestly for answers from his Word, we learn that trusting him, obeying him, and depending on him, brings joy and happiness.

---

[65] From a Sermon by Leo Harris, preached in a CRC Church. Circa 1950

When we are suffering, we cry out to God for answers. Many times, he gives us a reason, but some things we may not understand until we see Jesus face to face. Even then our questions will probably disappear, as Job's did when he was challenged by God (see Jb 42:1-6).

Meanwhile he is to us the God of all comfort -

> "Praise be to the God and Father of our Lord Jesus Christ, the Father of compassion and the God of all comfort, who comforts us in all our troubles, so that we can comfort those in any trouble with the comfort we ourselves receive from God. For just as we share abundantly in the sufferings of Christ, so also our comfort abounds through Christ" (2 Co 1:3-5).

How important it is for us to be totally dependent on God, and fully obedient to him. When we reach this point the Lord knows he can trust us to give him all the glory for anything we might do for him.

In his strength: In fact, everything we do from here on is done in his strength and not in our own.

Works of charity, such as feeding the hungry and caring for the widows can be offered up to the Lord as part of our worship to him.

Our daily tasks undertaken in caring for our family can be part of our worship, because doing these jobs to the best of our ability sanctifies them.

How this attitude changes our life: Tasks that before seemed to take away from our times with God now bring us into a new threshold of praise and adoration of his marvellous wonders. We discover that while we do repetitive work, we can be praising him, and if sometimes we cannot praise him with our lips, we can still be praising him with our spirit. In this way we can fulfil Paul's injunction to -

"Rejoice always, pray continually, give thanks in all circumstances; for this is God's will for you in Christ Jesus" (1 Th 5:16).

We must surrender to God: Jesus, our example, was completely surrendered to his Father's will. He said of himself: -

"By myself I can do nothing; I judge only as I hear, and my judgment is just, for I seek not to please myself but him who sent me" (Jn 5:30).

"I love the Father and do exactly what my Father has commanded me" (Jn 14:31b).

When we are completely surrendered to the Lord, every part of our life, spiritual or ordinary, brings glory to him. This was the apostle Paul's experience. His testimony was –

"I can do all this through him who gives me strength" (Ph 4:13).

When the Lord finds he can trust us he gives us work to accomplish for him.

John Calvin: He was one the Lord could trust with important work. Calvin was the second major founder of the European Reformation after Martin Luther and he became the father of Calvinism and the Presbyterian church. He wrote the renowned *Institutes of the Christian Religion*, plus collections of prayers, commentaries and sermons. He was influenced by Luther and suffered persecution for his new beliefs.

He was naturally shy but had to be bold and fearless in defending what he preached.

He and his wife, Idelette, did great things for God while suffering illness, weakness, and the death of their little ones. They were a product of their times and suffered ill health along with others who lived in their day.

John Calvin reached a place of surrender and his motto was "To God be the glory."

The surrender of John and Idelette to the will of God led them toward spiritual maturity. Our surrender to God and our dependence on him will lead us also into greater spiritual maturity.

We are a product of our times today; times that are certainly healthier than the time of Calvin, but we too can be taken through times of death to self to bring about the maturity God needs in us.[66]

This has been our experience: I asked my husband during one very trying period -

"How many of these death experiences do we have to suffer?"

His answer was classic –

"As many as are needed!"

In contrast to Calvin and other great men and women of God our own life task may seem humble and obscure, but it is still important to God.

We will continue to grow, and develop into strong Christians, if we remember these three life lessons.

- To live by the Word of God
- In the power of the Holy Spirit
- In obedience to the voice of God.

Learning the principles of surrender and obedience while we go through trials and testings will help us to gain a true balance in our Christian life.

---

[66] *This Was John Calvin* by Thea B. Van Halsema

Chapter Fourteen:

After God's Heart

Balancing our Christian life requires us to seek God with our whole heart, trusting and obeying him completely.

After God had rejected King Saul for his disobedience, the prophet Samuel told him -

> "But now your kingdom will not endure; the Lord has sought out a man after his own heart and appointed him ruler of his people, because you have not kept the LORD'S command" (1 Sa 13:14).

Samuel was talking about David, who was to be the new king of Israel. What did God see in David? I believe there were seven characteristics David showed by his life that pleased God.

David worshiped: He was a man who knew his God, and he knew how to worship him with his whole heart. Here is one of many instances -

> "Praise the LORD, my soul; all my inmost being, praise his holy name. Praise the LORD, my soul, and forget not all his benefits – who forgives all your sins and heals all your diseases, who redeems your life from the pit and crowns you with love and compassion, who satisfies your desires with good things so that your youth is renewed like the eagle's" (Ps 103: 1-5).

David was honest: He was honest and open about how he felt and spoke from his heart to God in his psalms of praise and worship –

"I cry aloud to the LORD; I lift up my voice to the LORD for mercy. I pour out before him my complaint; before him I tell my trouble...Set me free from my prison, that I may praise your name. Then the righteous will gather about me because of your goodness to me" (Ps 142:1-2; 7).

David was brave and resourceful: He did not hesitate to challenge Goliath, whom he overcame by using his skill with a sling – a skill he had gained by practising day after day while watching his father's flocks. He had used his sling to kill a lion and a bear and he knew he could kill Goliath also. There was no doubt in his mind that God was with him to give him victory.

David was a leader: He was a leader of men and they followed him faithfully -

"All those who were in distress or in debt or discontented gathered around him, and he became their commander. About 400 men were with him" (1 Sa 22:2).

David was wise. Despite the fact he had been anointed by Samuel to become king of Israel, David was careful not to go ahead of God's timing. He refused to hurt Saul, even though he had two opportunities to do him harm. This was because he was deeply aware that Saul was also anointed by God (1 Sa 24:1-7; 26:1-12).

David knew how to encourage himself in the Lord: (see Ps 143).

David also taught Asaph, his director of music, to encourage himself in the Lord. When he was in despair. Asaph cried out in his Psalm -

"I will remember the deeds of the LORD; yes, I will remember your miracles of long ago. I will consider all your works and meditate on all your mighty deeds" (Ps 77:11-12).

David knew how to repent and humble himself before the Lord: He repented sincerely and asked for forgiveness when Nathan, the prophet, accused him of adultery with Bathsheba, and the murder of her husband, Uriah the Hittite. (see 2 Sa 12:1-14 & Ps 51:1-19).

Jesus first: If we would also be a people after God's heart, then we can take note of David's character traits, but it is Jesus our Lord we must follow closely. He has sent his Holy Spirit to indwell us and to guide and direct us in our Christian walk.

Jesus must come first in our life: We discussed this truth in chapter one of this book –

> "Love the Lord your God with all your heart and with all your soul and with all your mind and all your strength" (Mt 22:37).

We must not be like the early Israelites of whom it was said –

> "They worshiped the LORD, but they also served their own gods in accordance with the customs of the nations from which they had been brought" (2 Kg 17:33).

The pattern of the children of Israel, throughout the Old Testament, was to serve God if they saw his miracles and wonders, but when a new generation came along that had not seen any of God's mighty works, they would fall away. God would then allow an enemy to attack them and they would cry out for rescue. When God answered them, by raising up a leader to free them from their oppression, they would return to God and his ways.

Some of these leaders were Othniel, Ehud, Shamgar, Deborah, and Gideon. They march courageously through the book of Judges.

This journey was repeated over many weary years until finally, under Ezra and Nehemiah, the Jewish nation was refined and ready to acknowledge their God as the only true God. Synagogues were set up, and the people listened gladly to the Word of God. This goal was reached by God's decree; for when the right time came, he was able to send Jesus into the world to begin his saving work, as many Old Testament prophets had foretold.

How can we know if Jesus is Lord of everything in our own life?

Here is a simple test: Is there anyone, or anything, that means more to us than Jesus our Saviour and his Kingdom of light?

Hindrances: If we would become a people after God's heart, we must remove any hindrance from our lives. We must have a single eye, a single purpose; to serve God, anything that hinders must be put aside -

> "Therefore, since we are surrounded by such a great cloud of witnesses, let us throw off everything that hinders and the sin that so easily entangles. And let us run with perseverance the race marked out for us, fixing our eyes on Jesus, the pioneer and perfecter of faith" (He 12:1-2a).

To be like Jesus: How well do we know him? What are the characteristics of Jesus we should strive to emulate?

His kindness: Jesus was gracious to the little children when the disciples tried to drive them away. He said -

> "Let the little children come to me, and do not hinder them, for the kingdom of heaven belongs to such as these" (Mt 19:14).

His sensitivity: He showed empathy to the woman taken in adultery -

> "Neither do I condemn you", he declared, "go now and leave your life of sin" (Jn 8:11).

His hatred of sin: He showed his righteous anger against the Pharisees, the Sadducees, and the religious leaders -

"Woe to you, teachers of the law and Pharisees, you hypocrites!" (Mt 23:13).

His love for sinners: He told the rich young ruler -

"If you want to be perfect, go, sell your possessions and give to the poor, and you will have treasure in heaven. Then come, follow me" (Mt 19:21).

His pity and compassion: Jesus' heart went out to the people -

When Jesus landed and saw a large crowd, he had compassion on them, because they were like sheep without a shepherd. So, he began teaching them many things (Mk 6:34).

His gentleness and humility: He said,

"Come to me, all you who are weary and burdened, and I will give you rest. Take my yoke upon you and learn from me, for I am gentle and humble in heart, and you will find rest for your souls. For my yoke is easy and my burden is light" (Mt 11:28-30).

His courage: He knew all the time what lay ahead of him and saw others crucified from time to time, yet he faced death on the cross with unflinching bravery.

His lack of partiality: He treated Judas the same as the other disciples. When he washed his disciple's feet Judas was included. It was only after this that Judas went out to betray Jesus.

His patience: He showed infinite longsuffering and kindness toward the disciples.

His purity: He was without sin.

His wisdom: Many times. he showed wisdom in answering the priests. On one occasion they asked him -

"Tell us then, what is your opinion? Is it right to pay the imperial tax to Caesar or not?"

But Jesus, knowing their evil intent, said, "You hypocrites, why are you trying to trap me? Show me the coin used for paying the tax". They brought him a denarius, and he asked them, "Whose image is this? And whose inscription?"

"Caesar's," they replied. Then he said to them, "So give back to Caesar what is Caesar's, and to God what is God's" (Mt 22:17- 21).

His forgiveness of the soldiers at the cross: -

"Father, forgive them, for they do not know what they are doing" (Lu 23:34).

Jesus did so many things:

- He preached the good news of the kingdom of God.
- He taught his disciples and others, including the seventy.
- He used simple stories and parables to explain the kingdom.
- He healed all who came to him in faith.
- He warned the religious leaders against their hypocrisy.
- He spent time with sinners.
- He spent time in fasting and prayer.
- He suffered and died for us all.
- He rose again in fullness of power to bestow the Holy Spirit on his followers.

These are some of the fascinating things you can discover about Jesus as you search the gospels; and to know a person, to love that person, is to become like that person.

Within the parameters of the will of God: How much like Jesus are we? We aren't all called to public ministry; God is content if we do what he has ordained for us according to our gifts and abilities, but Paul tells us we should seek to please him by our life (see Ep 5:10).

The resurrection power displayed by God is available to us, to overcome sin, to quicken our mortal bodies and to set us free to serve him.

Trust and obey: Those are two very important words if we would be after God's heart. This is what will give to us the overflowing joy of God.

> "Trust and obey for there's no other way
> To be happy in Jesus but to trust and obey"[67]

Are you miserable in your Christian experience; then sometime, somewhere, you have refused to obey the Lord. Seek his forgiveness and return and do the thing you feel God is asking you to do. Your joy will return.

Sharing Jesus' sufferings: Did you know that Paul knew he was going to suffer for the gospel before he began his ministry? (see Ac 9:16).

Even so he still went on to minister to the Gentiles and spread the good news of the gospel everywhere, despite his many sufferings (see 2 Co 6:3-10). Only the grace of God enabled him to keep going to fulfil God's will for his life.

We may not be asked to suffer like Paul, but we may suffer in other ways. We may suffer loss of friends and family or be scorned by contemporaries. We can endure fasting, go without sleep, have no-where safe to live, or perhaps live in a foreign land as a missionary.

---

[67] *Trust and Obey* by John Sammis; Redemption Hymnal

Suffering can be part of our human existence, but then there may be some who will never be required to suffer in any way at all. What God is looking for in us is a willingness to suffer for him, a complete abandonment of our life to him - that is if we are serious in our desire to be "after his heart".

To study the life of Jesus and to walk in his steps, seeking to please God in everything we do is another important foundation stone for a balanced Christian life.

Chapter Fifteen:

Character and Discipline

In this chapter we learn how to retain our joy in the Lord while we grow in character and discipline. Strengthening our character and learning the importance of discipline will go a long way toward balancing our life in Christ.

True joy: Years ago, I came across this saying.

> "Some Christians have only enough Christianity to make them miserable, but not enough for true joy."

This could be because they have not been taught adequately, or because they do not believe fully that they are forgiven and that they can approach the throne of God in prayer at any time. -

> "Let us then approach God's throne of grace with confidence, so that we may receive mercy and find grace to help us in our time of need" (He 4:16).

True joy comes from knowing deep down that we are loved and forgiven by God, and because of this we are willing to **obey** him in all things.

We read about this joy in the Psalms: -

> "You make known to me the path of life; you will fill me with joy in your presence, with eternal pleasures at your right hand" (Psalm 16:11).

And Paul exhorts us in Philippians: -

> "Rejoice in the Lord always. I will say it again: Rejoice!" (Ph 4:4)

As pointed out in the last chapter *After God's Heart*. We can lose our joy through disobeying the Lord in some way. If we do disobey, we can repent and return to obedience. Our joy will be restored.

How do we measure up? Are we completely loyal, faithful and obedient to God every moment?

For instance, would we be willing to lose our job because of our integrity? Do we obey the law when no one else but God can see us?

I remember going regularly to an early morning prayer meeting in downtown San Diego. At 5.30 in the morning no other cars were on the road, but I still stopped each day at the stop signs and waited patiently for the lights to change. This is a small illustration, there are many far more serious. If, for instance, you are responsible for the collection money for your church, or the money for the business where you work, are you careful to make sure always that no money is wasted or misused?

The test of love: We train our children to be loyal, faithful and obedient to us according to their age and understanding. God expects the same from his children also. Sadly, we do not always measure up to his standard.

Sin leads to spiritual death: The Word of God tells us that sin leads to death. Some sins are more harmful than others but all lead to the same terrible end -

> (People are) "tempted when they are dragged away by their own evil desire and enticed. Then, after desire has conceived, it gives birth to sin; and sin, when it is full grown, gives birth to death" (Ja 1:14-15).

Formation of character: It is the daily choices and decisions we make that form our character. Our actions can be good, but what about our reactions? It is those reactions that can be ruinous to our character. They can be jealousy, resentment, hatred, fear, or perhaps even self-pity These negative emotions we can hide from others, but they still affect our character.

Our outward actions can be good if they are thought about ahead of time, but it is our spontaneous reactions which are unplanned that reveal our true character.

Jesus said: -

> "What comes out of a person is what defiles them. For it is from within, out of a person's heart, that evil thoughts come - sexual immorality, theft, murder, adultery, greed, malice, deceit, lewdness, envy, slander, arrogance and folly. All these evils come from inside and defile a person" (Mark 7:20-23).

Christian character: When we accept Jesus as our Saviour and are filled with his Holy Spirit then begins a process of sanctification. At first, we struggle with sin as Paul explains -

> "I know that good itself does not dwell in me, that is, in my sinful nature. For I have the desire to do what is good, but I cannot carry it out. For I do not do the good I want to do, but the evil I do not want to do – this I keep on doing" (Ro 7:18).

Slowly as we continue to read and meditate on the Word of God, we begin to understand that we are set free from sin because of Jesus' death on Calvary and we start to lay hold of the victory he has won for us. We gain the revelation that we are set free from sin, we are no longer slaves to sin. We are set free from the compulsion to sin and now we can live a life of freedom from guilt. This fills us with joy and happiness and blessing granted to us by God through Jesus our precious Saviour.

This Word comes alive to us: -

"Therefore, there is now no condemnation for those who are in Christ Jesus, because through Christ Jesus the law of the Spirit who gives life has set you free from the law of sin and death. For what the law was powerless to do because it was weakened by the flesh, God did by sending his own Son in the likeness of sinful flesh to be a sin offering. And so he condemned sin in the flesh, in order that the righteous requirement of the law might be fully met in us, who do not live according to the flesh but according to the Spirit" (Ro 8:1-4).

Discipline is needed: -

"But I tell you that everyone will have to give account on the day of judgment for every empty word they have spoken" (Mt 12:36).

Empty words are careless words – "Not taking care or paying attention, unthinking, insensitive."

The foundation of all discipline must be love: In this we can follow the example of our Lord Jesus. He submitted to his Father willingly and it is important for us to follow in his steps, as the author of Hebrews advises us:

"Moreover, we have all had human fathers who disciplined us, and we respected them for it. How much more should we submit to the Father of spirits and live" (He 12:9).

Discipline is needed for character building: It is as we meet and solve problems through disciplining ourselves that we grow in character

This gives our life a wonderful new meaning. We learn to set short term and long-term goals so that we do not waste our time in this life of ours.

Then, if others will allow us to help them with their problem solving, we can assist them, with the Lord's help, to grow and mature in their Christian character.

Putting off rewards: You must first deal with the problems of your life, even though this may be painful, before allowing yourself the rewards of accomplishment.

Self-esteem: For children, good discipline takes time, and their self-esteem is built during one on one time with mother or father. "Quality" time cannot make up for "quantity" time. Consistent parental love gives children a deep internal sense of their own value, their security, and this helps them to cope with any problems they may face.

Recent experiments have pointed out how vitally important eye contact is between mother and baby while breast or bottle feeding and it has been pointed out that there is great harm in a mother being distracted from this important eye contact by looking at a television program or a mobile phone. There is a certain feeling of security that a baby gets from having their mother's undivided attention. Eye contact with the father is equally important. Could this be one of the reasons why young people feel so insecure and anxious these days?

For those who are adults, the feeling of being valuable is essential to mental health. A corner stone of self-discipline, it teaches us to value our time, so we do not continually put things off until tomorrow, thus procrastinating.

It has been proved that those over 60 years of age,[68] have far less problems in mental health than the under 60's. This is because most of the over 60's had a Judeo/Christian/Biblical foundation which included the Ten Commandments with a

---

[68] I am writing in January 2020.

belief in heaven and hell, as well as rewards for living a good life and an inevitable future punishment for wickedness.

It is my belief that humanism, with its denial of original sin, has done much harm to society. Humanism has not been good for the mental health of the average person.

Alain de Botton: This atheist, who has written a book about the idea of creating a special "religion" for atheists, claims that Christians, because of their beliefs, have better mental health than those who don't believe in God. He cited many Christian habits, such as meditation, forgiveness, and community, as being good for physical and mental health.[69]

Being responsible: The problem of distinguishing between what is our responsibility and what is not our responsibility is one of the great problems of life. We need to be careful we do not take on burdens that don't belong to us.

With great difficulty we learn this lesson. We cannot live another person's life for them, and we cannot make them do what we feel would be better for them. Watching your adult children going through a painful trial is one instance when you realise that you must step back. There is nothing you can do except be there for them if they reach out for help in their troubles.

Finally, with the Lord's help you must learn to say, "This is not my problem!" – always providing it truly is no concern of yours, not even in the sight of God.

Facing the truth: We cannot make wise decisions unless we see a situation clearly. It is hard to perceive problems distinctly when we are in the middle of a painful trial. Sometimes we can only think in a straightforward manner if we step back and view the problem from a distance. Then if

---

[69] *Religion for Atheists* by Alain de Botton.

we are given more information we must think carefully and, if necessary, change our plans to gain a better result.

Sometimes it is hard to see the truth and we tend to avoid reality when it is painful. We must have the discipline to overcome that emotional pain.

King David: He was one who chose denial instead of dealing with the truth in his family life. You can read the story in 2 Samuel chapters 13-19.

When David's son, Amnon raped Tamar, his half-sister, and ruined her life, David did nothing! This was a terrible crime as Tamar was denied marriage and children. In those days, and in that culture, no man would wed a woman who was not a virgin, unless she was a respectable widow.

Absalom: Who was Tamar's full brother, waited two years and then murdered Amnon for what he had done. (see 2 Sa 13:28).

David still did nothing!

Absalom fled and stayed away three years and then returned and waited two more years before he was allowed into the king's presence (2 Sa 14:33).

Full of bitterness Absalom planned carefully and then attempted to take his father's kingdom away from him. He finally died a traitor's death (2 Sa 18:9-18).

David was a loving father and, despite what Absalom had done, he mourned him bitterly, to the disgust of his military general Joab (2 Sa 19:1-7).

David denied reality and hid from the truth until forced by Joab to see it.

These terrible times for David fulfilled Nathan's prophecy. This was given after David had committed adultery with Bathsheba and murdered her husband, Uriah. This act of

David was particularly vile as Uriah was one of his mighty men, who had helped him win his kingdom (see 2 Samuel 23:24-39). Nathan the prophet accused David and warned him of future punishment -

> "Why did you despise the word of the Lord by doing what is evil in his eyes? You struck down Uriah the Hittite with the sword and took his wife to be your own. You killed him with the sword of the Ammonites. Now therefore, the sword will never depart from your house, because you despised me and took the wife of Uriah the Hittite to be your own" (2 Sa 12: 9-10).

Though God forgave David when he repented of his adultery with Bathsheba and his murder of Uriah, David still had to bear the terrible consequences of that sin -

> "The Lord has taken away your sin. You are not going to die. But because by doing this you have shown utter contempt for the Lord, the son born to you will die" (2 Sa 12:14)

We must remember this truth, even though God forgives a repentant heart we must still suffer the consequences of our sin. As when a person robs or assaults someone, even though they may ask forgiveness, they must still pay the penalty of a jail sentence.

Did David come from a dysfunctional family? Was this the reason for his denial of the truth? This is a possibility as his father presented seven of his sons to Samuel, one after the other, without thinking of David until Samuel said, "Are these all the sons you have?" (see 1 Sa 16:10b).

Another sign of dysfunction in the family was the anger of David's oldest brother when David arrived at the army camp and asked about Goliath. Eliab obviously despised David for some reason -

"Why have you come down here? And with whom did you leave those few sheep in the desert? I know how conceited you are and how wicked your heart is; you came down only to watch the battle" (1 Sa 17:28b).

Being the youngest of eight brothers could not have been easy; we can only imagine the bullying that David may have endured.

This dysfunction could have been the reason David denied reality and did nothing to punish Amnon, and then later, Absalom.

Acknowledging the truth: Sometimes it is hard to see the truth when you are suffering emotional pain. Help is needed from a counsellor or mature Christian friend to learn what is true and to face the truth. Once the truth is faced healing can begin. Just knowing the truth can set you free to heal.

The balancing act: On each occasion, when faced with a problem, we must either delay the reward we desire, or on the other hand, be ready to work toward a solution if that will not cause more problems.

On one hand we must assume total responsibility for ourselves. But, on the other hand, we must realise we are not responsible for other adult persons.

On one hand we must be truthful. On the other, we must be careful when helping others not to speak before that person is ready to hear what we have to say. The Holy Spirit can help us be tactful and wait for the right time to speak.

Self-discipline is enlarging and character building:

The four methods of discipline are inter-related, and used at different times, but love is the underlying motive for learning how to strengthen your own character and then to help others.

Learning the way to true joy by understanding how to overcome sin helps us in our life experience, while building a strong character through discipline, guarantees that we will indeed lead a more balanced Christian life.

Chapter Sixteen:

The Pillars of Solomon

A deep understanding of what, "security" and, "stability" mean brings us to our last foundation stone for gaining a life of balance in this world in which we live.

Solomon, the son of David, was the king permitted to build a Temple to take the place of the Tabernacle that had served the Israelites for so long -

> "For the front of the temple he made two pillars which together were thirty- five cubits long, each with a capital five cubits high. He made interwoven chains and put them on top of the pillars. He also made a hundred pomegranates and attached them to the chains. He erected the pillars in the front of the temple, one to the south and one to the north. The one to the south he named Jakin and the one to the north Boaz" (2 Ch 3: 15-17).

Reading this passage in the Message Bible, I was struck by the names of the two pillars that Solomon erected in the front of the temple he built for the glory of God. The Message Bible gives the meaning of these two names. In the Hebrew, Jakin translates as *Security* and Boaz translates as *Stability*.

How aptly these two words encapsulate the Christian life that we are called to live, as we work out our salvation carefully day by day. Paul the apostle pointed this out to the Philippians -

> "Therefore, my dear friends, as you have always obeyed – not only in my presence, but now much more in my absence – continue to work out your salvation with fear

and trembling, for it is God who works in you to will and to act in order to fulfil his good purpose" (Ph 2:12-13).

Security: Our security is sure. If we have accepted Jesus as our Saviour, then the Apostle John tells us that we are safe in his great love -

"For God so loved the world that he gave his one and only Son, that whoever believes in him shall not perish but have eternal life" (Jn 3:16).

We are secure in his forgiveness of our sins: -

"If we confess our sins, he will keep his promise and do what is right: he will forgive us our sins and purify us from all our wrongdoing" (1 Jn 1: 9 GNB).

"He does not punish us as we deserve or repay us according to our sins and wrongs. As high as the sky is above the earth, so great is his love for those who honour him. As far as the east is from the west, so far does he remove our sins from us" (Ps 103:10-12 GNB).

We are secure in our hope of eternity: -

"May the God who gives us peace make you holy in every way and keep your whole being – spirit, soul, and body - free from every fault at the coming of our Lord Jesus Christ. He who calls you will do it, because he is faithful" (1 Th 5:23-24 GNB).

We are secure in God's love: -

"See what great love the Father has lavished on us, that we should be called children of God! And that is what we are" (1 Jn 3:1a).

The security of our salvation and the hope of eternal life give us a solid secure base on which to build our life. Then no matter what happens on our journey we will never turn away from our Lord because we will trust him through triumph and tragedy, through valleys of sorrow and mountain tops of joy and victory. Nothing will move us from our testimony.

Stability: In this 21st century there is a great dearth of stability. We face the breakdown of the family and the constant instability of the nations who seem to be continually at war. Because of the abandonment of the Judeo/Christian ethic and the teaching of humanism we face a breakdown in character and in family life. Paul warned us this would be a sign of the last days -

> "But mark this: There will be terrible times in the last days. People will be lovers of themselves, lovers of money, boastful, proud, abusive, disobedient to their parents, ungrateful, unholy, without love, unforgiving, slanderous, without self-control, brutal, not lovers of the good, treacherous, rash, conceited, lovers of pleasure rather than lovers of God – having a form of godliness but denying its power. Have nothing to do with such people" (2 Tim 3:1-5).

The lack of strong Christian leaders: We need leaders who will band together and speak with strength against the madness of political correctness and the multiple expressions of gender reorientation that have gripped our youth.

Hopefully, both these aberrations will begin to turn around as people of good sense agree together to bring sanity back into the public forum.

We need religious leaders to put aside their differences and to agree together to speak up against the tide of evil that is engulfing our world. If they had spoken up immediately the evil rot began then evil would not have such a grip on our society today.

The lack of strong, honest politicians: We need men and women of character to lead us week after week with the ability to decide on, and pass, decent laws for the good of all.

Domestic violence is on the increase with one woman in Australia dying each week through the brutality of the partner who should be loving and cherishing her.

> "The man who hates and divorces his wife," says the LORD, the God of Israel, "does violence to the one he should protect," says the LORD Almighty (Mal 2:16).

> "Each of you also must love his wife as he loves himself, and the wife must respect her husband" (Ep 5:33).

Terrorism and child trafficking: We face the horror of terrorism with innocent people dying cruelly with no warning, and the crimes against little children, such as child trafficking, paedophilia, sexual abuse, cruelty, and even murder -

> Jesus said, "Let the little children come to me, and do not hinder them, for the kingdom of heaven belongs to such as these" (Mt 19:14).

Jesus said also to his disciples -

> "Things that cause people to stumble are bound to come, but woe to anyone through whom they come. It would be better for them to be thrown into the sea with a millstone tied around their neck than to cause one of these little ones to stumble" (Luke 17:1-2).

As Christians we must be very different, portraying a Christian character which shows the fruit of the Spirit (see Ga 5:22-23).

We must display a character which is honest, ethical, and can be trusted, based on the security we have in Christ; stable lives that cannot be moved from the good news of Jesus and all that he accomplished for us.

Christians dying for their faith: I recently heard that presently, on average, there are eleven Christians dying for their faith each day! Our prayers should be rising constantly to the Lord to give those dying the strength to endure. Who knows if and when someone we know and love may face death because of their belief in Jesus Christ, our Saviour.

It is time to stand up and be counted: We, as Christians, should pray and believe for a great revival of the fear of God. This would turn the people of our land back to a gentler time of honesty, purity, courage and unselfishness.

It is time for men and women of steadfastness and determination to bring about change in our land. Men and women who will not give up until fairness again is part of our culture. Laws governing equality need to be passed that will result in all citizens receiving a decent wage; enough to provide a home and comfort for their family.

If this does not come about then the future looks bleak. The rich will continue to get richer and the poor will continue to go without until a tipping point is reached, and society collapses into anarchy and chaos. If that happens then many will suffer before equilibrium is restored.

Christian stability: Steady Christians are those who are moderate, and stable in their beliefs. Having examined scripture thoroughly and come to a good balance of what it means to be a Christian, and how they should live, they are then able to share their faith with others sincerely and with enthusiasm.

There are some Christians who become fascinated by Bible prophecy and are continually trying to second guess what God intends to do next, despite the words of Jesus that even he did not know the day or the hour of his return.

Certainly, we are to look eagerly for the coming of Jesus and it is true that we can sense that time may be near. But over the centuries many others have been convinced of his soon return, yet we are still waiting.

One thing we can be sure of is that God is in control and everything will work out in his timing. This does give us security and stability no matter what happens. We live in exciting times and we should be praying for God's will to be done on earth as it is in heaven.

Transhumanism: Because of the increase of knowledge in the realm of artificial intelligence there is an uncertain future facing our children and grandchildren. In discussion with Martin Hamilton-Smith, a retired politician, I asked,

"What is the future of artificial intelligence.? How will it affect our lives? Will mankind become part robot, part human?"

His answer amazed me. He said -

"Aren't we already becoming part robot? Think of glasses, hearing aids, knee and hip replacements and a pace - maker to keep our heart beating. It is only a small step from these to brain implants to assist us in learning a new language. The possibilities are endless."

What does the future hold? Robots, because of their ability to connect to each other will soon exceed us in knowledge and ability. Only God knows what the final result will be.

One thing I am sure of. Only those Christians who are strong in the Word of God and strong in prayer will be able to remain stable and sure in their faith, able to make wise decisions for their future in this increasingly complex culture in which we live.

Only those will be secure and stable, able to remain balanced in their Christian experience, until they go to be with Jesus, or until he comes in the clouds to gather them to himself. What a wonderful time that will be!

There are many ways we can ensure our Christian life remains balanced and secure. We have discussed many of them in this book. I pray that you will be able to grasp hold of these thoughts to assist you to keep a balanced and stable Christian experience.

A closing prayer: -

> Give me faith for my doubt
> Strength for my weakness
> Joy for my sorrow and
> Stability for my emotions
>
> Let me glory in your Might
> Filled with awe at your Majesty
> Open to your love and light
> Washed with your Word
>
> Give me songs of worship
> A heart filled with gratitude
> Giving thanks to you Father
> For your everlasting love.
> Amen (AMC)

Bibliography

Ai, Paul Dr. *From Witchdoctor to Apostle*. Hampton, Virginia: Vision Outreach International.

Barclay, William. (1963). *New Testament Commentary*. Edinburgh: St. Andrew Press.

Baxter, J. Sidlow. (1952). *Explore the Book*. Volume Four. Marshall, Morgan and Scott.

Benner, David G. & Hill, Peter C. (1999). *Baker's Encyclopedia of Psychology & Counselling*: Baker Books.

Botton, Alain de. (2012). *Religion for Atheists*. Hamish & Hamilton.

Chant, Barry. (2012). *Living in the Image of God*. Tabor

Chant, Alison. (2006). *Divine Healing, The Wonder and the Mystery*. Vision Publishing.

Chant, Ken. (2015). *Strong Reasons*. Vision Publishing.

------------- (2000). *Discovery*. Vision Publishing.

Daniell, David. (2001). *William Tyndale. A Biography*. Yale University Press.

Doige, Norman MD. (2007). *The Brain That Changes Itself*. Viking Press.

Halley, Henley H. (1965). *Halley's Bible Handbook*. Grand Rapids: Zondervan.

Halsema, Thea B. Van. (1959). *This Was John Calvin*. Grand Rapids, Michigan: Baker Book House.

Henry, Matthew. (1953). *Matthew Henry's Commentary*. Marshall, Morgan & Scott.

Hill, Napoleon. (2005). *Think and Grow Rich*. The Ralston Society. New Edition.

Hinn, Costi W. (2019). *God, Greed and the Prosperity Gospel*. Grand Rapids: Zondervan.

Howard, Kevin & Rosenthal, Marvin. (1994). *The Feasts of the Lord*. Nashville, Tennessee: Thomas Nelson Inc.

Hurnard, Hannah. (1986). *Hearing Heart*. Wheaton, Illinois: Tyndale House.

Jensen & Payne. (1997). *Finding God's Will for Your Life*. Sydney, Australia: Matthias Media.

Layard, Austin Henry. *Nineveh and Its Remains*. Cambridge University Library.

Liardon, Roberts. (2000). *God's Generals. Healing Evangelists*. Whitaker House.

Lipton, Bruce H. Ph.D. (2016). *The Biology of Belief. Unleashing the Power of Consciousness. Matter & Miracles*. Carlsbad, California: Hay House Inc.

Moyer, S. Elgin. (1982). Revised and enlarged by Earle Cairns. *The Wycliffe Biographical Dictionary of the Church*. Chicago: Moody press.

Moore, David. *The Shepherding Movement*; https.//www. Good reads.com/book.

Morison, Frank. (1968). *Who Moved the Stone*. London: Faber & Faber.

Peale, Norman Vincent. (1967). *Enthusiasm Makes the Difference*. A Fawcett Crest Book.

Pearsall, Paul P. (1998). *The Heart's Code. Tappimg the Wisdom and Power of Our Heart Energy*. Pearsall.

Porter, David. (1986). *Mother Teresa, The Early Years*. Marylebone Rd., London: SPCK. Holy Trinity Church.

Redemption Hymnal. (1958). *Rock of Ages* by A. M. Toplady & *Trust & Obey* by John Sammis. Elim Publishing Co. London.

Robinson, Stuart. (2004). *Mosques & Miracles*. Upper Mt. Gravatt, Qld. Australia 4122: City Harvest Publications. P.O. 6462

========== (2017). *The Hidden Half*. P.O. Box 6462. Brisbane, Qld. Australia: Chi Books.

Schroeder, Gerald. (1977). *The Science of God*. Sydney: Free Press.

Slemming, C. W. (1955). *These are the Garments*. Fort Worth, Pennsylvania: Christian Literature Crusade.

Tenney, Merril C. (1975). General Editor. *The Zondervan Pictorial Encyclopedia of the Bible*. Grand Rapids: Zondervan.

Tozer, A. W. (1961). *The Knowledge of the Holy*. New York: Harper One. Harper Collins.

Vine, W. E. (1969). *Expository Dictionary of New Testament Words*. Oliphants.

Webster's. (1980). *New Collegiate Dictionary*. Springfield, Massachusetts: G & C Merriam Co.

Yancey, Philip. (2006). *Prayer, Does it Make Any Difference*. Hodder & Stoughton.

Journal Articles

Christianity Today. art. *Joke Van Opstal:* August 2000

Ministries Magazine. art. *Beware of Counterfeit Spiritual Gifts*: Spring 1985.

Reader's Digest. art. *Secrets of Olympic Heroes* by Jeff Bond.

Youtube Articles

Khulman, Kathryne: Quote from an article in YouTube.

Sumrall, Lester; *My Relationship with Smith Wigglesworth*: YouTube

www.ingramcontent.com/pod-product-compliance
Lightning Source LLC
Chambersburg PA
CBHW061302110426
42742CB00012BA/2018